CONSIDER YOUR *Call*

Consider Your Call

Gisela Yohannan

BOOKS

a division of Gospel for Asia

www.gfa.org

ISBN: 978-1-59589-036-8

Published by gfa books, a division of Gospel for Asia
1800 Golden Trail Court, Carrollton, TX 75010
1-800-WIN-ASIA

Printed in the United States of America

For more information about other materials, visit our website: www.gfa.org.

07 08 09 10 11 12 / 7 6 5 4

TABLE OF CONTENTS

DEDICATION

This book is dedicated to the students of our Gospel for Asia Bible colleges in Asia. I am tremendously excited to see the Lord calling so many young people to enter His harvest fields.

ACKNOWLEDGMENTS

There are a number of people the Lord has placed in my path without whom this book would not have been possible. I will always be grateful, for each one had a special part in seeing this book come to pass.

Krissy formatted the manuscript numerous times and helped make it look just right. My dear friend Heidi edited and entered the book on the computer. David also helped type in some chapters. And the entire staff of Gospel for Asia faithfully prayed for me as I wrote and rewrote.

My children, Daniel and Sarah, have been the source of many of my learning experiences and also of great blessing. My husband, Dr. K.P. Yohannan, graciously read through the manuscript and offered valuable insights.

But most of all, I want to offer thanks to the Lord Jesus Christ. I was 14 years old when He called me to serve Him; and He has been absolutely faithful to lead and guide. I pray that this book and my life will continuously be my offering of thanks to Him.

INTRODUCTION

When the Lord calls us to serve Him, it is just like the start of a foot race. We are excited, full of strength and ready to run. However, a short while down the track, we discover that it takes more than our initial excitement if we want to last for the next 20, 30 or 50 years. And it takes even more to finally cross the finish line and win the prize.

The purpose of this book is to help us consider and understand our calling and then find the courage and strength, through God's grace, to endure until He has finished His purpose through us.

Surely there will be no greater joy for us than one day to exclaim, like Paul: "I have fought the good fight, I have finished the course, I have kept the faith" (2 Timothy 4:7).

My prayer is that the Lord will use this book to help you serve Him with all your heart and all the days of your life.

Gisela Yohannan

PREPARED
BY
Him

1

GOD'S CALL TO EVERY BELIEVER

Contrary to what you may think, God has no favorite children. He does not specially select some to whom He passes out His gifts and calling, making the rest just second class, without much significance for His kingdom.

Jesus loves and regards the littlest sheep of His flock just as much as He does His mightiest apostle. In His eyes, the job He assigns to His tiniest sheep is as great a calling as leading a church with 10,000 people.

We often have difficulty in grasping this. We look at someone with a full-time ministry call almost jealously at times. We think he must be holier, more blessed and definitely more loved by God than we are.

But let me ask you this: How do *you* know that you don't have a full-time calling as well?

Perhaps your answer is something like this: "I have never felt any burden or desire in my heart to teach and preach, go to Bible school or be involved in a Christian ministry. When altar calls are given for dedication to full-time ministry, I have never had any 'tug' on my heart to respond."

Dear friend, I believe you when you say this. But did you know that along with your salvation, you automatically received a full-time call to be a Christian, a follower and a witness for Jesus? This call applies 24 hours a day, seven days a week, and is effective until death!

God never intended for you to be a part-time Christian—in the morning for family prayer, on Sunday for church services and perhaps on Wednesday for Bible study.

Whether you work in a bicycle shop, hospital, your own home or your neighborhood, you have a full-time call to be a witness and to represent Christ at that place. The only reason God hasn't called you to be a pastor or evangelist is because He desperately needs a full-time witness at the marketplace, in the train station or in that office building. You could have qualified for any job in God's kingdom, because God does not rely on our wisdom or abilities but rather on His Spirit to indwell and direct us. But He needs you where He has positioned you.

When you recognize and accept the fact that God has called you to be a full-time witness *before* you are anything else in this life, this will have great consequences for the rest of God's kingdom.

A PART OF GOD'S BLUEPRINT

The reason Jesus left His disciples on earth and sent them into all the world was to build His kingdom in a territory ruled by sin and controlled by Satan.

Building God's kingdom is just like building a house. Before you start, you need a blueprint, materials and a work crew. The work crew ranges from skilled professionals such as carpenters, brick layers, painters and plumbers to water carriers, cement mixers and load bearers. Each of these people is absolutely needed to be able to complete the building.

God also has a blueprint for building His kingdom in India,

Bhutan, Tibet and around the world. When you look very closely at the blueprint, you will find your name as a believer there.
God has assigned a specific part of His kingdom to be built just
by you.

You must realize that nothing—absolutely nothing—in your
life is an accident. God created you with your specific part of
the blueprint in mind. Everything in your life has been preparation for you to be able to fulfill this specific task in God's plan.

Just think: your upbringing, your trials, your education or
lack of education, your culture, your abilities, your brown or
yellow skin, your citizenship, even your being born as a man or
a woman—all this was necessary to make you into a skilled work-
man for your assigned task.

Looking at our lives in this way, we can truly say: "And we
know that God causes all things to work together for good to
those who love God, to those who are called according to His
purpose" (Romans 8:28).

I Am Called for My Part, Not Yours

It is very important for us to remember that whether we
are in full-time ministry or placed as a full-time witness in our
neighborhood or business, we are there for fulfilling our own
part of the blueprint. We should not try to covet or do someone
else's job.

I remember a time when one of my friends visited me in my
home. When she spoke of my husband's constant travels, she
commented to me: "I often think about you. I could never do
what you do."

My answer to her was this: "You are not supposed to do what
I do. God has called you for something else. God gives each of
us grace for our own calling."

This is truly my experience. Whatever God has assigned to
you on His blueprint, He will give you sufficient grace to fulfill

exactly that. Remember, you have been prepared by Him to be a craftsman, skilled for your area of that blueprint.

FULL-TIME MINISTRY VERSUS FULL-TIME WITNESS

You might be ready to do your job, but in your heart you might feel that others, especially those in full-time ministry, have much better tasks assigned to them than you seem to have.

God has kept the distribution of jobs and calling to His own authority. We cannot change that part. But we can joyfully do whatever He asks of us with all our hearts. Jesus said that if we are faithful with a few things, He will put us in charge of many things (Matthew 25:21).

Let us look at a few people in the Bible who didn't have a full-time call like Peter, James or John did, but whose service within their professions was absolutely necessary to fulfill God's plan for His own Son as well as to fulfill many prophecies. If each of these people would have been involved in anything else than their regular job, they would not have been useful for God's purpose.

> > > > >

When Jesus was born in Bethlehem in the stable, his mother Mary had no place else to put her newborn baby than in a manger, a feeding trough for animals.

In the Christmas story and in our Christmas songs, we read and sing about the angels, the star, the shepherds and the wise men. But we never mention the man who made this manger. He must have been a professional carpenter or stonecutter, depending on whether the manger was made with wood or hewn out of stone.

All his life, this man worked hard at his job. Perhaps he often thought: "I wish I could be like the rabbi in our synagogue. If I had his job, I could *really* serve the Lord God of Israel, whom I love with all my heart. I just make these old mangers for other people's stables. What kind of life do I have?"

But can you imagine the honor and the privilege this man had to make that manger to welcome the Son of God, the Creator of the universe, into this world? God chose this man, in his profession and at his workplace, to be part of the fulfillment of prophecy. The rabbi down the street, a full-time teacher of the law in that synagogue, never received that same high honor and privilege.

❯ ❯ ❯ ❯ ❯

Just before the end of Jesus' ministry, He was in Bethany at the house of Simon, along with His disciples. As they were relaxing at the table, Mary came in the room. She broke an alabaster vial containing very costly perfume, which she poured over Jesus' head and feet. Throughout the centuries, Mary has been remembered for her special deed of anointing Jesus for His burial.

But for a moment, let us forget Mary and instead look at that costly perfume. Only a professional could blend and mix these expensive spices together to produce such a perfect ointment, one that cost 11 months' worth of wages.

We don't know who this perfume mixer was. His name is not recorded here on earth, but I am sure he is known in heaven. He might not have ever realized when he made the perfume Mary later bought, that he was specifically chosen by God Almighty to use his art and skill to provide this precious ointment to prepare Jesus for His death to save a lost world.

❯ ❯ ❯ ❯ ❯

And then there was a simple weaver who made bath towels for people. What a boring job it must have been, day in and day out, weaving these towels. I am sure this weaver sometimes wished he could make those beautiful robes and clothes with nice colors and decorations worn by the rulers and kings in their palaces. But no, he was stuck at his job weaving those plain, ordinary towels.

Little did this weaver know that Jesus needed one of his towels to teach His disciples one of the highest principles of the heavenly kingdom: "But the greatest among you shall be your servant" (Matthew 23:11).

During the Last Supper, Jesus washed His disciples' feet and dried them with the towel that this unknown weaver made at his daily job. If this weaver could have known that his towel would be used by the Son of God Himself, he would have been so excited and happy to be the one to make it possible, because of his profession, for Jesus to do such practical teaching.

> > > > >

There was also a carpenter who must have felt quite depressed, because he had the worst job in the whole world. He was assigned by the Romans to make crosses for executing criminals. Surely, he thought, there couldn't be a more awful job than the one he had.

I am sure he often wished he could make beautiful furniture for people's homes instead. At least that would be something useful and appreciated. But making crosses was a very unthankful, cursed task.

As this carpenter did his work, one day he made a cross that was picked up by some Roman soldiers and laid on the back of Jesus, the Lamb of God, who was about to be slain for the sins of the whole world.

Jesus had need for this cross. The whole purpose for Him to come into this world was to die, so salvation could be given to everyone who believed in His name. This carpenter's service was needed by God to make it possible for Jesus to die for a lost world. He was part of the prophecy in Isaiah 53 that described Jesus' death, and he was also part of the triumph over sin, death and the grave.

> > > > >

Dear friend, your name is on God's blueprint for building His kingdom. He needs your obedience and faithfulness in order to fulfill His plan through you as a full-time Christian witness at your workplace or in your neighborhood. You are needed by the living God. If you allow Him to use you, your service can be as fruitful and effective as someone else in full-time ministry.

If you decide, however, that because your job is rather small or insignificant it therefore doesn't matter if, how and when you plan to do it, please consider these consequences:

1. *God's plan (His building) won't be completed on time, and you will become a hindrance for God's purpose for your village or nation.*

2. *You will delay others' work.* For example, the roofer is unable to put the roof on the house unless you are completely finished with the wall you were assigned to build. In a church situation, this means that your pastor cannot preach the message God gave him for your unsaved neighbors and relatives, unless you first do your job and invite them to the meeting.

3. *If you don't have a willing heart for your task, God will be forced to find someone else to shoulder your responsibility.* This means that someone else will have to work a double shift and perform a task he was not specifically prepared for as you were.

As you read this book and my words about full-time ministry, please don't put it down, thinking that it doesn't apply to you. Almost everything that applies to those in full-time ministry will apply to you as well, because you have received a full-time calling to be a witness for Jesus as long as you live.

GOD'S CALL
TO
FULL-TIME
Ministry

> › › › › ›

A young couple had been attending our prayer meeting for quite some time. One day they announced to the rest of us that they were going to leave for Bible school the next month.

We were astonished by their sudden decision. To our amazement, we learned that they had visited a preacher who was supposed to have a gift of prophecy in order to find God's will for their lives. They had to pay 1,000 rupees to get an audience, and at the end of their visit he gave them a prophecy. He told them that God had called them into the ministry, and so off they went. I never heard what happened to them later.

I believe that buying an answer like this is quite a dangerous way to determine the course of your life. However, I also understand this young couple. They must have grown tired of waiting, praying and seeking for God's will. They wanted to end their search and start *doing* something with their lives.

I have met many other young Christians who wonder whether God has called them or not. In Part II, I would like to share a few things I have learned about God's call to full-time ministry.

➤ ➤ ➤ ➤ ➤

2

IT HAS TO BE GOD
HIMSELF WHO CALLS YOU

*S*ome years ago, a Bible school invited me to come and speak to their ladies' class. The girls and I had a wonderful time together. I decided to ask them a few very personal questions:

"Why are you here? Did you come here because your parents sent you? Do you attend the school for the purpose of gaining greater Bible knowledge? Are you here because you hope to marry a pastor and this education will give you a better chance at a proposal? Is your husband a Gospel worker, and he has told you to attend some classes? Or, did God call you to serve Him?"

All of the above reasons may be valid ones to attend a Bible school, but only the last one is good enough to enter full-time ministry. I say this with all seriousness. You will *not* make it as a pastor, missionary or Bible woman if your call is based on any of these:

> Your parents' wish or their vow to God when you were born

> The agreement of your church and teachers who feel that you have a lot of talent

› Your ability to speak publicly and your intelligence in
  your studies

› Your own wish to do something for God

› Your compassion for lost and suffering people

Compassion is wonderful, abilities are great, and parents'
fervent prayers and desires to see their children serve the Lord
are the best thing that can happen to them—but none of these
is a call.

You see, once you are in the ministry, storms will inevitably
come. In fact, the powers of darkness will declare war against
you. It will be impossible for you to face suffering, self-denial
and persecutions with no real call on your life. God *Himself*
has to be the One to call you; otherwise, you are headed for
trouble.

One of the most beautiful stories in the Bible is the story of
Hannah. She had vowed to God that if He gave her a son, she
would give him to the Lord all the days of his life, and no razor
would come on his head. This meant that she would see to it
that his life was set apart from the world. She was serious with
her promise, and God was gracious to her and gave her a son.

Hannah had told her husband about her vow, and he didn't
stop her, which he had the right to do according to the law.

When their son Samuel was born, she told her husband
about the plan she had for him: "I will not go up [to Jerusalem
for the yearly sacrifice] until the child is weaned; then I will
bring him, that he may appear before the LORD and stay there
forever" (1 Samuel 1:22).

Elkanah replied to his wife, "Do what seems best to you.
Remain until you have weaned him; only may the LORD confirm
His word" (v. 23).

Elkanah was the spiritual leader of his family, and as such
he was responsible to watch that whatever his family did lined

up with Scripture. He respected his wife's love for the Lord, her promise to God and her enthusiasm to give their child to Him.

But he also clearly recognized that a vow on her part was not enough foundation for an anointed ministry. In his answer to Hannah, we can see that his single concern was that God's call and confirmation had to be there. Otherwise, their son would head off into a self-proclaimed ministry.

Hannah and Elkanah did not know when and if this confirmation would come. Yet they seemed to have great faith that God would hear their prayers on behalf of their son.

The day that Samuel was brought to the temple was not the day God confirmed His word. Samuel's preparation by his parents was excellent. He willingly stayed with Eli. His heart was right, and his service was faithful and dedicated. First Samuel 2:26 says this about him: "Now the boy Samuel was growing in stature and in favor both with the LORD and with men."

These were good signs and brought joy to his parents, to Eli and to God; but this was not God's call and confirmation yet.

It was several years later that God Himself called Samuel at night. For the first time he heard God's voice, and that night the Lord entrusted a prophetic message to him. He was chosen to become God's spokesman to Eli and to the nation of Israel.

GOD'S CALL IS A CLEAR CALL

No general can fight a war with soldiers who don't know whether they are enlisted in the army or not.

It is in God's best interest that we know His will for our lives. There is no advantage to His kingdom if we walk around doubting whether He has called us or not.

When we look at the Bible, we can see that God called people in such a clear way that later on, none of them ever turned back to question whether God really called them or not. Along the way, they may have doubted their abilities, their qualifications, their worthiness, their courage and even God's love or care—but never their call.

Let's look at some of the ways that God called His prophets, kings, apostles and disciples.

When God called **Abraham,** He addressed him personally: "Now the LORD said to Abram, 'Go forth from your country, and from your relatives and from your father's house, to the land which I will show you' " (Genesis 12:1).

Gideon was told by an angel, "Go in this your strength and deliver Israel from the hand of Midian. Have I not sent you?" (Judges 6:14).

When **David** was chosen as king, God said to the prophet Samuel, "Arise, anoint him; for this is he." Samuel anointed David in the midst of his brothers (1 Samuel 16:12–13).

The day the Lord commissioned **Jeremiah,** He told him, "Before I formed you in the womb I knew you, and before you were born I consecrated you; I have appointed you a prophet to the nations. . . . See, I have appointed you this day . . ." (Jeremiah 1:5, 10).

God called some of them by name. Just think about **Moses** at the burning bush (Exodus 3:4), **Samuel** in the tabernacle (1 Samuel 3:10) and **Paul** on the road to Damascus (Acts 9:4).

Jesus called some of His **disciples** with the words "Follow Me," and He made sure they heard it (Matthew 4:19, 9:9).

For each one, God's approach was different; but by the time God was through talking to them, they clearly knew that He had called them to full-time service.

There are endless ways in which God can call us: through reading a scripture or a Gospel tract, an altar call, hearing an audible voice, a song, seeing a vision, going through a trial, hearing a sermon, talking to a person, a prophecy that God confirms in our heart, visiting a mission field, hearing the voice of the Holy

Spirit speaking quietly in our heart, or a growing awareness of His claim on our life.

In whatever way He chooses to call you, you will know that He means you.

For example, God called my husband at the age of 16 during a mission conference. He had heard reports from the pioneer fields and the challenge that was given. When he was all alone later that night in his room, God began to call him to give his life for missions. After a struggle that lasted several hours, he surrendered himself and accepted God's call. This call was clear enough to cause him to travel 2,000 miles to North India for mission work instead of going back home. The call was also clear enough to enable him to serve the Lord for the past several decades.

When the Lord called me, I was 14 years old and had only been saved for two days. It wasn't in a church or during an altar call. I was walking on the road with some friends. One of them asked me what I was going to do later on in my life. At that moment, I knew in my heart that the Lord wanted my life for missions. The call of God in my heart was so clear that I never once considered anything else.

Looking at my own experience, the only thing with which I can compare the clarity of His call to serve Him is the clarity of His call to repentance and salvation. I had no doubt at all that He meant me.

What Should You Do if You Have Doubts?

God is not angry with us if we don't understand His call right away or if we have doubts. Often we are just learning how to distinguish His voice among all the other voices surrounding us.

God loves us and He knows that we may not have had much practice in hearing Him call us. What He did for Samuel, He will do for us as well.

In 1 Samuel 3:3–10, God called Samuel by name, but Samuel thought it was Eli. We find the reason in verse 7: "Now Samuel did not yet know the LORD, nor had the word of the LORD yet been revealed to him."

After Samuel went to Eli three times, the old priest told him that it must be the Lord. He instructed Samuel how to respond if it should happen again. Sure enough, God called a fourth time during that same night; and this time Samuel knew it was the Lord and responded to His voice.

This account shows us something very important about our God: He loves us enough, and He has enough patience with us, to call again and again until it is totally clear who is calling us.

So we must not be afraid that God might only call once and if we don't recognize His voice immediately, our chance is up. Believe me, He will not move until we get His message.

Here are some reasons why we might not recognize His call at first.

We all have heard or read fantastic testimonies from people whom God called through a heavenly vision, a light shining into their room or an audible voice speaking to them. Perhaps they were knocked down like Saul on the way to Damascus. Our problem is that we often wait for such a dramatic event to happen and ignore the still, small voice with which God is trying to speak to us.

Another problem could be that somehow we think that if God is really calling us, He would reveal more details right away in addition to a simple "Follow Me." We want to see the whole road map, not just the first step.

If you have doubts, take time to seriously seek the Lord with all your heart. You might want to fast as well. Maybe there are some godly people who will pray for you and with you.

One more thing: If someone has a prophecy for you, *wait* for the Lord to confirm it to you before you make any major moves.

Please remember that God wants you to know His will clearly. He will not tell someone else and leave you out.

You can also join a summer outreach with a Gospel team. This will give you an opportunity to search your heart and test what you think might be a call.

Remember, God is faithful, and He has promised that if we seek Him we will find Him.

GOD'S CALL IS FOR A SPECIFIC TASK

God has a plan for His kingdom, and when He calls you, He wants to incorporate you into this plan. He may tell you exactly what it is right from the start, but more often, He will only reveal one step at a time as you go along. When you say "yes" to God's call, you cannot expect instant revelations of His plan. You will enter a life of learning to listen, praying for guidance, trusting step by step, seeking His will and learning to rely on the Holy Spirit.

The plan He has for you might seem great in your eyes. However, it may not look glorious at all. In fact, you might even be disappointed when you see what it is. (I have already talked about this in Chapter 1.) I want you to know that His plans for you might cost you everything you have, everything you hoped for and even your very life.

If you surrender to God's call, you must also unconditionally accept whatever plan God has in mind for you, even if you don't know it yet. If you do not totally surrender to the lordship of Christ *without reservations*, your call will not have any meaning for God's kingdom. In fact, you will become a constant hindrance.

GOD ALWAYS WAITS FOR AN ANSWER

When God calls someone, He always waits for an answer. He will not go ahead with His plans until He hears from us.

Samuel's answer was "Speak, for Thy servant is listening" (1 Samuel 3:10). When Samuel said "Thy servant," we see clearly that he surrendered himself to God's will.

Isaiah said, "Here am I. Send me!" (Isaiah 6:8). Even though he didn't yet know the message, he declared that he was willing to be the messenger.

James and John didn't say anything, but we see their clear answer by what they did: "And they immediately left the boat and their father, and followed Him" (Matthew 4:22).

Paul said, "What shall I do, Lord?" (Acts 22:10). When he addressed Jesus as "Lord," he not only acknowledged Him as God, but as his master and his owner who had all the rights to his life, and he was willing to receive His orders.

God gives us the option to say, "Yes, I accept" or "No, I decline." If we say "no," we may regret it later in life, and surely in eternity. Often God in His love continues to speak to us for some time, asking us to change our minds. But if we insist on our "no," He has to pass us by and look for someone with a willing heart.

God gives us a chance to count the cost before we accept His call. The cost is clearly outlined in the Bible.

> If anyone wishes to come after Me, let him deny himself, and take up his cross daily, and follow Me (Luke 9:23).

> If anyone comes to Me, and does not hate his own father and mother and wife and children and brothers and sisters, yes, and even his own life, he cannot be My disciple. Whoever does not carry his own cross and come after Me cannot be My disciple (Luke 14:26–27).

> No one of you can be My disciple who does not give up all his own possessions (Luke 14:33).

> Be faithful until death, and I will give you the crown of life (Revelation 2:10).

Your answer is not a joke! It is a lifetime commitment that you make before God Himself and the whole spirit world. Heaven and hell are witnesses!

3

AFTER YOU HAVE
ANSWERED GOD'S CALL

*P*erhaps you surrendered to the Lord's call after a time
of personal struggle, fear and confusion. Now your
heart is finally at peace. You are overjoyed, knowing
that you are in the center of God's will.

You can't wait to announce your decision to your family,
relatives, friends and fellow believers. You are so sure they will
rejoice with you, encourage you and even help you along to go
to Bible school and eventually to the mission field.

You wait until evening for everyone to be home, and then
you tell them about your great decision. As you share your story,
you are once again overwhelmed by the grace of God to entrust
to you such a high calling.

By the time you are finished, though, your father's face has
become dead serious. Your mother is weeping, your sister walks
out of the room and your two younger brothers are afraid to say
even one word. You are confused, and you try to figure out why
everyone seems so upset when you have just shared the most
important and wonderful experience in your entire life.

That night your father calls for his brothers to come to your home for a family council. They talk for a long time, and then they call you into the room. Your father's oldest brother addresses you:

"Son, we appreciate your faith in God. But you must give up this plan you have for Gospel work.

"You know very well that our family is poor. We do not have much farmland, and our homes have mud walls and thatched roofs. For many years now, your father has sacrificed greatly to send you to school and give you an education.

"You are our only hope for improving our family situation. Look at your mother, and how hard she has to work. She is getting older now—doesn't she deserve to have it easier?

"Think about your sister. If you don't get a job and earn money, she has no chance at all to get married. Even if we all help together, we will never be able to come up with the dowry money that is needed.

"Your younger brothers have no chance for a higher education if you don't help them. Both of them are so bright and could become engineers or doctors, but without you they have no hope.

"Son, our family needs you. There are others who can do Gospel work. Surely God doesn't want you to neglect your parents or disobey them.

"This is our plan: We have a family friend who is a doctor in Europe. We received a letter from him just two days ago offering you a good-paying job in the hospital where he works. He will pay your airline ticket, and you can stay with him once you get there.

"Tomorrow we will send him a telegram notifying him that you will be able to come within a month. If you still want to do some Gospel work, you can do it later when you come back in a few years. You can always witness to people at your job or in your spare time."

➤ ➤ ➤ ➤ ➤

Maybe the members of your family are non-Christians, and they didn't like your conversion at all. It was a shame to their family name and a great concern to the whole village whether the gods would be angry now and send punishment.

After the Lord called you, it took a lot of courage to tell them that you were going to go to Bible school. You expected them to be angry, but you are totally unprepared for their reaction.

They tell you that if you go ahead with this plan of yours, they will disown you and denounce you as their son. You will no longer be allowed to live in their home or ever come back.

➤ ➤ ➤ ➤ ➤

A week ago, you met with the pastor and the elders of your church. You shared with them about God's call to the North Indian mission fields and that you want to prepare yourself and go to Bible school.

Because you come from a Hindu background, you can't expect any help from your home. You asked the church if they could help send you to Bible school. You were quite sure they would, because everyone likes you and you have been very active in the youth ministry and in Sunday school.

Today you received their answer. They have decided to pay for all your expenses if you promise to come back after Bible school to work with your own church and denomination right here at home where you are needed. However, if you want to go on to a mission field, you can't expect any help from the church.

➤ ➤ ➤ ➤ ➤

You are a young woman, and Jesus has put His call on your life to reach out to the many lost and suffering women and children in the slums and among the tribals. Today, you have decided to approach your parents to ask permission to go to Bible school.

As you enter your home, you notice that everyone is excited and smiling. They can't wait to tell you the good news: a proposal for you just came from a very respected family in the community. Their son is a lawyer and has his own firm. His family are people of integrity, and they are also well-to-do. Your parents and relatives would be so happy for you to marry this young man.

Of course, they love you and will leave the choice with you, but they are absolutely sure you will accept the proposal. You know very well what this marriage would mean to your family: the chance of a lifetime to step up in society.

While everyone else is extremely happy, you go to your room and you feel frightened. Somehow, you need to find enough courage to tell your parents that you can't marry this man, because God has just called you to serve Him and He has a different plan for your life.

> > > > >

Perhaps your family members are dedicated believers, and they agree with your plans to go into full-time service. They pray for you and are willing to support you as much as they can.

But since you have surrendered to God's call, it seems that so many unexpected difficulties are in your path: your bicycle breaks down, your father loses money in his business and your brother who works the family farm becomes seriously ill. It looks as though you will be forced to postpone your plans for a long time.

HEAVEN IS FOR YOU—HELL IS AGAINST YOU!

Why am I writing about all these difficulties that you could encounter after you have answered God's call to serve Him?

Because this is reality.

As soon as you have decided to serve the Lord, you can count on disappointments, difficulties, temptations and situations that seem to gang up on you to make you miserable, to change your mind, to lead you into sin or to slow you down in your pursuit.

What has happened all of a sudden? You have entered a war zone. You have become a prime target for the enemy! He knows that if he can stop you now he doesn't have to deal with you later on the mission field, when you are stronger and actively involved in destroying his kingdom.

At this point I want to caution you: Please don't make the mistake of accusing your parents or home church by telling them that the devil is using them to hold you back or that they are selfish and unspiritual.

Love them anyway, even in their lack of vision and their inability to trust in God's provision. Forgive them in your heart and keep yourself free from bitterness. You don't help them or change their minds by arguing, talking behind their backs or accusing them.

Just quietly start your walk of faith, trusting in the One who called you. He will never leave you nor forsake you.

It might take years for your family to understand your decision. They might even feel that you have deserted them in their great need or that you have dishonored their name.

This will be one of the most difficult decisions you will ever have to make—to trust God to provide for your family and to walk away from them, leaving them behind with hurt feelings and tears.

This is only the beginning of a lifelong battle. Because of this, as I wrote earlier, you will never make it unless God Himself has called you.

Our examples in the Bible had to face the same struggles. As soon as they were called by the Lord and stepped out in faith to follow Him, they encountered opposition and warfare.

When **Abraham** left his homeland and arrived in Canaan, God promised him that He would give this very land to his descendants as an inheritance. The next thing we read of is a famine in Canaan, so severe that Abraham left for Egypt.

After **Jacob** had his life- and heart-changing encounter with the angel of God and his name was changed to Israel, the very next thing that waited for him was an army led by his brother, Esau.

David was anointed as king. However, the next step was not a crown on his head but a life-and-death encounter with Goliath. Saul himself, recognizing David's call to the throne, pursued him and tried to kill him as long as Saul was alive.

Jeremiah, Isaiah and many of the prophets through John the Baptist were called by God in a great way. As soon as they accepted their call, they quickly discovered that they risked their lives every time they opened their mouths.

God had just started to speak to **Joseph** through dreams that **Joseph** himself didn't even understand yet. However, his brothers hated him because of those dreams, and the next thing he knew, he was thrown in a well and sold to Egypt as a slave.

Jesus was baptized in the Jordan River. God had just endorsed Him as the Lamb of God, and He was ready to enter His ministry. But before He had preached even one sermon, He faced a series of the most severe temptations of His lifetime.

The apostle **Paul** had given his life to Jesus and accepted his call to serve Him on the road to Damascus. After his amazing conversion, he faced immediate persecution by the Jews. Not only that, when he tried to associate himself with the Christians in Jerusalem, they were afraid of him and avoided his fellowship.

Stephen entered his ministry as a deacon in Acts 6:5. By verse 12, he was already framed and arrested, and in chapter 7, he was martyred.

As much as the enemy is against you, you must realize that all heaven is for you! Believe, confess and count on this: "Greater is He who is in you than he who is in the world" (1 John 4:4).

He is well able to bring you through. He will walk with you, even if you are left alone by all others. He will stand by His Word, and He will give you courage and strength that you never knew before or even thought possible.

You Are Set Apart by God

You might feel lost among the masses of people in India, and your life might look very insignificant, especially if you live in the slums or among tribal people who have little access to the opportunities enjoyed by others. However, in the eyes of God, you are very important, and He is keenly interested in you. Psalm 139:1-18 is the most beautiful description of the intimate involvement our Heavenly Father has with every human being He has ever created and the total knowledge He has about each one.

In His foreknowledge, God knows what your life will be, and He knows the decisions you will make. He already knows from eternity past the exact date and moment when you will receive Jesus as your Savior and when you will surrender to His call to serve Him.

In God's heart, He set you apart for His purpose long before you were born. We can see this in several instances in the Bible in which God revealed to the parents of a child yet to be born that their son was already set apart to serve Him in a special way. Examples of this are **Samson** (Judges 13), **John the Baptist** (Luke 1:11-23) and **Jesus** (Matthew 1:18-21; Luke 1:26-38).

In each case, the purpose of God for such a revelation was to give special instructions to the parents regarding the name of the child, special upbringing and the purpose of his ministry. Samson was to become a judge, John the Baptist would be the forerunner of the Messiah and Jesus would be called the Son of the Most High and Redeemer.

It was obviously important to God that the parents had the right mind-set toward the future of their child and, with it, that they would provide the right environment, protection and preparation for their child's calling.

Most of us probably discover only when God calls us that He must have set us apart long ago.

Jeremiah made this discovery the day he was called to be a prophet. God said to him, "Before I formed you in the womb I knew you, and before you were born I consecrated you; I have appointed you a prophet to the nations" (Jeremiah 1:5).

The moment that Samson's, John's and Jesus' parents received their instruction from God on how to raise their children, they became absolutely responsible before God to take His instruction seriously and do exactly as they were told.

Abraham, Jeremiah, David and the many others we read about in the Bible became accountable for their separation by God at the moment He revealed His will for each one of their lives. In the same way, when God calls us to serve Him, we become responsible for the fact that God has set us apart for His purpose.

You Must Set Yourself Apart for Him

From the moment you knew about your call and accepted it, God expected you not only to acknowledge that He had set you apart for His purpose, but that you in turn would set yourself apart for Him. He waits for you to consciously become separated unto Him and His purpose for your life by laying down everything else such as your plans, wishes and dreams for your future and the pull of the world with all its attractions.

It also means you must take special care of your spiritual development: a Christlike character, obedience, sensitivity to hearing God's voice, recognition of His guidance and learning to open your heart to the teaching of the Holy Spirit.

All this does *not* just fall on you automatically. It only starts to develop when you *deliberately* set yourself apart and then make it your lifelong practice to walk with God.

It is vitally important that just as He has set us apart in His plan, we must also set ourselves apart for Him. If we fail to do this, we will easily become sidetracked by our desires and by the world around us, and we jeopardize our readiness.

Over and over we read this phrase in the Bible: "When the time was fulfilled . . ." It clearly shows that God has dates and exact times when His plan, or part of it, goes into effect.

You are on such a timetable in God's plan. He has marked dates and hours when you are supposed to act on His Word and fulfill certain tasks assigned to you. Believe me, your spiritual growth must exactly match the task you are called to accomplish. It will not if you do not give special attention to your development and readiness.

Your problem may be, at this point in your life, that you are very young in your faith and you have no experience, no guidance and not much understanding of God's ways. The Bible is still full of major mysteries and difficulties, and you don't know where to turn for direction.

If you are in such a situation, pray that the Lord will give you an understanding pastor or mature believers who can give you godly counsel. Read and study the Word diligently. Study the biographies of godly men and women, and draw on their wisdom and advice. Entreat the Lord to teach you through His Holy Spirit. In whatever area the Lord gives you light and understanding, live it. If you live by the light He gives you, it will naturally lead to more light.

I was saved and called by the Lord during a two-week youth vacation held by a church that was 350 kilometers from my village. It was impossible for me to attend that church more than maybe once a year. In addition, I was very shy and not at all used to sharing my heart with anyone.

When I returned to my home, I had so many questions about my salvation as well as everything else. I decided to write them in a letter to the pastor who had led me to the Lord. A few days later he replied, and I was so grateful. He and his wife continued to pray for me. Whenever I had trouble with my new faith, I wrote another letter. He always wrote back within two or three days—I could count on it. He would share Bible verses, correct me and give me advice.

When I told this pastor that the Lord had called me for missions, he took it very seriously. One day he wrote some advice in his letter that became the greatest help for me in making the right choices and decisions. This is what he wrote: "Your call must come first in your life, above everything else, including job, friendships and marriage."

I accepted his advice, and I began to consciously live with it in mind. I discovered it to be the best protection from traps, sins and detours.

Practically, this meant for me that everything needed to line up with and further this call; otherwise, I must gladly give it up, regardless of the cost. This principle determined the places I would go, which friendships I could have, how I would spend my time, what I allowed my eyes to see and even my future plans for marriage.

I remember well the yearly high school parties and functions our whole class was required to attend. Part of the program didn't line up with the convictions I had about my life and call. Knowing the embarrassment I would cause myself, I refused to participate in certain activities as the only one in my class.

My father took me and my sister to some of the social events of his club. It was important to him that we would be well-equipped to move within our society according to Western culture.

One night, on the way home from such an event, I sat in the backseat of our car, looking out the window and thinking about the evening. It had been fun.

At that moment, the Lord began to speak to me in my heart. He said, "If you take part in this kind of lifestyle, it will take away your interest from Me and from your call. Your heart will be divided."

Right there in the car, I made the decision to no longer go to these social events so my heart could focus on the purpose for which God had called me. I was not even 15 years old then, and I remained firm in my decision, even if it was impossible for my family to understand some of my new "ideas."

Later, at nursing school, I had two roommates. They were nice, but their lifestyles and principles were not the same as mine. Among other things, both read magazines that were quite worldly and questionable. Because they left stacks of them on our table, I also began to look at those pictures and read some of the articles.

Again, the Lord reminded me that I must put my call first in my life, and therefore, I could not allow my mind to be filled with those things. That day, I decided that I would not touch those magazines again; and by God's grace, I didn't, even though they sat around our room for the next three years.

Because I had to consider God's call first, I knew I never could marry an unbeliever, just a "normal" believer or even a pastor. The only person I could marry would be someone whom God had called for foreign missions. That eliminated almost everyone. I was aware that I had to walk so carefully—I couldn't waste my life. I had to wait for God's choice and be willing to stay alone rather than make a fatal mistake and jeopardize my call.

Paul wrote to Timothy, "Guard what has been entrusted to you" (1 Timothy 6:20).

God actually entrusted Timothy with many things. One of these was his call to the ministry. The job of guarding, according to Paul's writing, was obviously not just heaven's business but very much Timothy's as well!

In the same way, your call is entrusted to you, and *you* must guard it. How can this be done? Accept safety limits, such as the advice I received, or set them up yourself. Believe me, it is hard enough to learn to be guided by the Spirit. Safety limits and boundaries are a great help to keep us going in the right direction.

From experience, I can tell you that the knowledge of God's call on my life and my decision to put it first became the greatest protection for me as I grew up, waiting for the day when I could finally leave my home and begin to carry out the plan He had for me.

YOU WILL LIVE A SEPARATED LIFE

Your acceptance of God's call and purpose for your life will lead you to live a separated life. I *don't* mean that you will begin to act or talk strangely or go to the jungle to become a *sadhu*. No, you are the same person, living in the same hut, wearing the same clothes and going to the same school or workplace.

But you feel it—something has happened inside of you. You have become aware of God's call, and with that awareness, your goals and interests will shift. In fact, your call will become your only goal. Very soon you will begin to evaluate everything you do in the light of your call.

You will find yourself different today than you were yesterday. As you look at the people walking down the streets of your village, your heart will be gripped by their lostness. You feel something burning in your heart and tears running down your cheeks.

You will look at your friends with whom you used to share so much in common, and now you feel almost like a stranger. Very soon you will start to even act differently. When your friends sit around just to talk and waste time, you no longer find the desire to join them. Instead, you will be somewhere on your knees praying for God's anointing. Instead of joining them when they play, you will study God's Word every chance you can get. When they make plans to earn a lot of money, you will find yourself kneeling beside your bed, weeping and entreating the Lord for lost souls. When they want to go places, you will desire more than anything else to be among God's people and in His house.

Oftentimes it will be harder for your family and friends to deal with you and to understand you because they knew you to be so completely different than you are now. They might feel irritated or even unloved as a result of your new behavior. In their eyes, you have become a religious fanatic because you no longer care for the fun times you used to have together with them. You may feel very lonely because no one around you seems to share or understand your deep desire for God.

You must be sensitive and careful that the people you love don't end up feeling totally rejected by you. By being sensitive, I don't mean that you should compromise your commitment. But you must do all you can to show them extra love.

YOUR CALL WILL CONSUME YOU

One of the clear signs that you truly have God's call on your life is that the inner knowledge of this call will not decrease but grow with every passing day. You can't shake it off or forget about it. In fact, your awareness of God's call will grow to the point at which it will consume you.

It will become all you think about and your only interest. Nothing else anyone could offer you—job, money or position—will satisfy you. Many nights you will not be able to sleep, but you will ponder instead about the years to come.

Your tears, your prayers, your highest hopes and your greatest longing will be to follow this call and to fulfill God's plan for your life.

You will become so conscious of God's call that it will be before your eyes day and night. It will be your first thought in the morning when you wake up and your last thought before you fall asleep at night. You will walk down the street, sit in the classroom at school, wait for the bus, work in the field, cook at the stove in your kitchen or wait at the intersection for the traffic light to turn green, and it will not leave you.

I remember so well how, many times at school, I found it hard to concentrate on the lectures of my teachers because my mind would wander off to the mission field and the years ahead.

YOU CAN'T WAIT TO GO

Some of us receive our calls at a time in our lives when we are able to go immediately to Bible school, learn under a pastor or start a ministry.

But if God calls you as a child or as a young teenager, chances are that it will be years before you can actually go to the mission field. You need to finish school and at least reach the minimum age in order to be accepted in a Bible school. Some mission organizations might have additional requirements, depending on what kind of ministry you will be doing.

I often used to sit down with a sheet of paper and count out how many more years, months and days I had to wait until I could go. I would write something like this: "Three years to finish high school, one year of home economics school [which was required in order to enter nursing school], three years of nursing school [most mission organizations I knew of in my country required a social profession], then Bible school, then the mission field."

It was such a long list, and I was thankful for every year, every month and every day that went by. I was longing so much for the day when I could finally start doing *something*.

After three years of nursing school, graduation day finally arrived. Everyone in my class was excited about their future positions in the local hospital, but my bags were already packed. I graduated in the morning, and in the evening I left. Three days later, I traveled to Switzerland to join an Operation Mobilization team for its summer outreach.

My parents and my friends told me, "You have studied so hard for three years—now you should at least work for a year to have some experience and to earn some money. Even if you don't want to do that, at least stay home for a few months or weeks to rest after all your exams." But my answer to them was, "I have waited for this day for so many years, and I can't wait any longer. I must go now."

There are several things that are very important to remember as you wait for the day when you are free to go.

1. *Don't allow or tolerate anything to come into your life that could cause you to lose sight of your call or hinder your readiness and availability.* Don't allow yourself to become ensnared by the love of the world, by going into large financial debts that would tie you down for years to come or by friendships that hinder your growth. None of these things is worth it. Get rid of them, give them up, throw them away. Keep yourself separated unto Him alone.

2. *Be careful that you don't live so much in the future that you are no good for the present.* If you don't take your present job, your school or your responsibilities seriously, you can easily hurt your testimony and the name of the Lord.

Take Jesus as your example and learn from His life how to

deal with the time you have until you can go. When Jesus was 12, He knew that He needed to be in His Father's house, yet He had to wait 18 more years, until He was 30, before the Father told Him, "Now the time has come."

What did He do in the meantime? Luke 2:51 says that He was in subjection to His parents. According to the traditions of that time, He must have done carpenter work like Joseph. Jesus had the most important call in the universe: to redeem fallen mankind. Yet His Father expected Him to be faithful at what He did until it was time.

3. *Prepare yourself.* Preparation for your ministry does not start the day you enter Bible school or when you preach your first sermon. It starts the moment after you have accepted God's call to serve Him!

Don't just look for special seminars or conferences. View *everything* that God allows to come your way as part of your preparation. You see, God wants to build your character and develop the fruit of the Holy Spirit in your life: "But the fruit of the Spirit is love, joy, peace, patience, kindness, goodness, faithfulness, gentleness, self-control" (Galatians 5:22–23).

Unless that happens, all the knowledge you accumulate in your head will not do much good. God wants depth in your life, and a Christlike character that portrays Jesus before the world without any words.

Read and study the Bible as much as you can. Memorize Scriptures. Read books, especially biographies. Make notes when you hear others preach and teach. Pray much.

Witness, pass out tracts and take part in the outreach of your church. Attend your church faithfully. Help and support the efforts of your pastor and the leadership of your church in whatever way you can. Be willing to do any kind of service, such as cleaning the church, setting up chairs, carrying literature, running errands and so on.

Be faithful in small things! Encourage others. *Rejoice* in learning to be a servant. Gladly do anything the Lord allows you to do. Remember, if He plans to make a leader out of you, He will teach you first how to be a servant.

GOD'S ANOINTING WILL BECOME EVIDENT

If God's call and anointing is upon your life, you don't have to fight and argue to prove to people that they should listen to you or give you a chance to preach in their church. In fact, you don't have to tell anyone. People will recognize God's call on your life because it will become evident that the Lord is with you.

Joshua took the leadership of the children of Israel after Moses' death. Surely he must have wondered whether the people would accept him and if he could ever live up to their expectations, because they would undoubtedly compare him with Moses.

In Joshua 1:5 God promised Joshua: "Just as I have been with Moses, I will be with you; I will not fail you or forsake you."

Then when Joshua and the people of Israel stood before the Jordan River, the Lord told Joshua, "This day I will begin to exalt you in the sight of all Israel, that they may know that just as I have been with Moses, I will be with you" (Joshua 3:7).

God took it upon Himself to endorse Joshua's ministry and to show everyone that indeed Joshua had God's call and anointing on his life. This definitely became evident to all when the Jordan River parted and Israel crossed over on dry ground, just as Joshua had told them it would. We read the result in Joshua 4:14: "On that day the LORD exalted Joshua in the sight of all Israel; so that they revered [feared] him, just as they had revered Moses all the days of his life."

Samuel didn't have to proclaim to all Israel that he had been called to be God's prophet. Nor did his parents or Eli have to go door to door and convince people. Everyone recognized it, because it was God who had called him and who personally saw to the publicity on Samuel's behalf.

We read this in 1 Samuel 3:19 and 20: "Thus Samuel grew and the LORD was with him and let none of his words fail. And all Israel from Dan even to Beersheba knew that Samuel was confirmed as a prophet of the LORD."

David the shepherd boy was anointed by Samuel to be the next king of Israel. In 1 Samuel 16:13 we read, "And the Spirit of the LORD came mightily upon David from that day forward."

People around David couldn't help but recognize it. When Saul was looking for a musician to calm him down, he was told by a young man: "Behold, I have seen a son of Jesse the Bethlehemite who is a skillful musician . . . and the LORD is with him" (1 Samuel 16:18).

All of Israel first saw the evidence of his anointing when David killed Goliath; and from then on they saw it continuously, because in everything David did, the Lord was with him.

> And David was prospering in all his ways for the LORD was with him. When Saul saw that he was prospering greatly, he dreaded him. But all Israel and Judah loved David, and he went out and came in before them. And it happened as often as they went out, that David behaved himself more wisely than all the servants of Saul. So his name was highly esteemed (1 Samuel 18:14–16, 30).

In the New Testament we see the same thing. Whenever God called and anointed someone, God Himself did the advertisement for their ministry, by confirming the words they spoke with signs and wonders.

> Therefore they [**Paul and Barnabas**] spent a long time there [in Iconium] speaking boldly with reliance upon the Lord,

who was bearing witness to the word of His grace, granting that signs and wonders be done by their hands (Acts 14:3).

When **Peter and John** were arrested after healing the paralyzed man at the temple gate in the name of Jesus, they were on trial before the elders and scribes. The moment they spoke, even their enemies could see their anointing. We read this in Acts 4:13:

> Now as they observed the confidence of Peter and John, and understood that they were uneducated and untrained men, they were marveling, and began to recognize them as having been with Jesus.

When you realize that you don't need to convince people about your call and qualifications for the ministry, you will have peace in your heart, even if they ignore you and don't give you a chance to prove it. God will confirm you. Walk humbly with the Lord, and He will exalt you, in His time. That is His promise in James 4:10.

I remember a brother who had God's call on his life. After finishing Bible school, he joined a Gospel team. He immediately wanted to be a leader. He expected others to recognize his superior ability to preach and his qualifications to make decisions. He desperately wanted others to respect him; therefore, he was dissatisfied with the simple accommodations he had and that he was supposed to use a bus for transportation.

Within one day of visiting an outreach led by an older evangelist, he was passing judgment over this brother's methods. He never considered the fact that the older brother had been a pioneer worker for more than 20 years, that he had established quite a number of churches and that he had won hundreds of people to Christ.

I also met a sister who had talent in so many areas that she was more qualified for leadership than all the other girls on her Gospel team. Her method of trying to prove to others that she should rightfully be in charge was by complaining to her team members about their present leader. She would constantly point out that she knew much more than her leader and that she was not given the respect that she deserved according to her abilities.

If God has called you to serve Him, these two examples probably illustrate the most destructive ways for you to begin your ministry and to be recognized as the Lord's servant!

Having this kind of approach and attitude, even secretly, clearly testifies of a heart filled with pride. In that case, you force God to break you before He can ever use you. James 4:6 tells us, "God is opposed to the proud, but gives grace to the humble."

According to this verse, God will have no other choice but to humble you; otherwise, you cannot qualify for any job in His kingdom.

4

GOD'S CALL TO
A WOMAN

I believe there are basically two ways in which God calls a woman to serve Him full-time:

1. *A clear call to her to work as a lady missionary*

2. *A call her husband has received that automatically includes her*

In many Asian cultures, the truly effective way to reach the women, who often live very restricted and secluded lives, is for another woman to go and share Jesus with them.

If the girl the Lord has called to such a ministry is unmarried, she should work under the leadership of a church, a mission work, a team of sisters, an older Bible woman or a married couple who is in the ministry.

This is very important for the name of the Lord as well as for her reputation, protection and acceptance in the culture in which she serves. It is good if she is bold and fearless in sharing the Gospel, but she must be very sensitive to consider the rules of her society; otherwise, her efforts will be hindered and her message rejected.

If the girl wishes to get married, she must clearly tell her parents and her pastor that she will only be able to accept the proposal of a Gospel worker—otherwise, her service for the Lord might be over!

In some cases, it might be very difficult for the parents to give their consent, especially if they are unbelievers. However, prayer can change their hearts, and the Lord is faithful.

If God calls a married woman, she definitely needs to get permission from her husband to visit other villages and work with a team. If he doesn't allow her to go, she should joyfully witness wherever and whenever she has the opportunity. She should ask the Lord to send people to her door; and she will be surprised how many will come her way.

She should *not* nag her husband, condemn him, talk negatively at church about his attitude or neglect her care for him. On the contrary, she should treat him with respect and pray diligently that the Lord will change his heart. If he sees how she treats him with so much extra kindness and love, his heart will be touched and changed by her godly attitude.

This advice was given by Peter to ladies who had unbelieving husbands (1 Peter 3:1-6). However, it works equally well if they are believers and need a change of heart.

Perhaps one of the more complicated cases is when a married man receives God's call to serve Him and he has a wife who is a believer, but she has no interest or desire to serve the Lord.

I have met brothers like this, and I feel deeply sorry for them. They are very lonely in their hearts, and they are forced to bear the burdens of their ministry without encouragement or support from their wives.

These men actually have to fight the devil on two fronts: first on their mission field and then at home. There is no question that their last bit of strength will be absolutely drained when they come home and all they can look forward to are complaints and family problems. Not only will this be an added hardship, but it will discredit the ministry in the eyes of everyone around them.

Whatever reasons these women have to resent their husbands' calls, they will not be considered valid in God's sight.
You see, according to Genesis 2:4, God does not look at a couple
as two separate beings, each pursuing their own lives. No, He
brought them together to be one unit. This means "together" in
every way—physically as well as spiritually.

As women, whether we like it or not, God has created us to
be helpmates to our husbands. This means that our God-given
purpose as wives is to help our husbands in all that God has
given them to accomplish. Therefore, when a husband is called
to full-time ministry, his wife is automatically included in this
call as his helper! Eve was included in God's plan for Adam's
life, as Sarah was included in God's purpose for Abraham. God
didn't even ask for Eve's or Sarah's consent! Because they were
married, when He gave orders to their husbands, He expected
the wives to start helping fulfill their husbands' calls.

To be automatically included as a helper does not mean at
all that a wife should take up fixing cars, farming or preaching
just because it's her husband's call or purpose. It means, first
of all, for her to be in total agreement with her husband and
submitted in her heart to him. Second, it means that she must
support and help him in every way she can.

As the wife of a Gospel worker, her call to help will include
prayer and emotional support for her husband. She will help
bear his burdens. Perhaps it will mean extending hospitality,
learning to counsel or teach a class, going with him from door
to door, being joyful and encouraged when things get tough
and being willing to suffer alongside him. Most of all, her job
must be to help her husband succeed in fulfilling God's call.
God will reward her along with her husband, as He did with
Sarah, because they are working as one.

If a wife rejects her husband's call, it might be that she
doesn't understand her purpose to be a helper or that she has

a serious misunderstanding about the lordship of Christ in her life. Helping her will perhaps take some teaching, patience, extra love, wisdom and much prayer on her husband's part. To be forced into submission or into accepting a call will not produce any good fruit. God needs to do the work in her heart as her husband intercedes on her behalf.

5

FINDING GOD'S CHOICE

*I*f you are preparing for the ministry, the choice of your marriage partner is the most crucial one of your entire life, next to your salvation. A wrong decision in this area can severely cripple your future service for the Lord, whereas a right one can multiply your effectiveness many times over.

As believers, we know that our Heavenly Father has a plan for each of our lives. If this plan includes marriage, then it will also include His choice of partner for us and the right time to make this commitment.

All of this sounds wonderful and spiritual, but how is it possible to know practically which person you are supposed to marry?

Please know this: Whether you live in a culture where your parents select your mate or you live in one where this is your own responsibility, God is well able to work through any human system to accomplish His purpose.

Above all, you must seek God's direction and guidance for your decision. Don't just start praying when you are ready to get married. You should start years earlier, if at all possible. Pray for your future wife or husband, that God will prepare you for one another and for your ministry together. Pray for each other's protection, purity, commitment to the Lord and for your future family life.

During the past few years, some of the young people in my husband's family have wanted to know my opinion on some of the marriage proposals they received.

I really don't feel qualified to judge a person's heart, especially after seeing him or her only one time and at such an official occasion. Most of the time at these proposal talks, my impression was that the young people involved were very intimidated by all the relatives staring at them, and they were scared and anxious about behaving and saying just the right things expected of them.

On a few of these occasions it seemed that the girl's parents would answer all the questions directed to their daughter. I only hoped that in her heart she felt exactly as her parents represented her. It would be a tragedy for her future life if her parents only said these things on her behalf in order to make the proposal a success.

If you have a call to serve the Lord and you are still unmarried, I would like to share some advice with you that I gave to some of the young people in our family and our Bible schools.

Before you ever look for a wife or a husband, *first* find out what you want to do with your life, and *then* look for a marriage partner who will match your vision. Don't ever plan to marry someone with the hope of changing his or her attitude or commitment to the Lord or the ministry afterward. It will not work, at least not apart from a miracle by God Himself.

After my husband and I were married, he told me that a number of years before when he started to pray for his future wife, he made a list of seven specific qualifications she needed to have in order to match the vision God had put in his heart for his ministry. I am glad that I only found out about the list *after* our marriage! However, if you have a clear picture in your mind of the type of person you should pray and wait for, it is definitely a great help in making such an important decision.

If you are a young lady, know that you will have to be prepared to lay down your own plans in order to help fulfill your husband's call. However, if the Lord has entrusted you with a call to a specific mission field, pray for someone whom the Lord has called to serve there as well.

If a proposal comes for you, you must have the courage to tell your parents and anyone else involved with this responsibility how you believe God wants to use your life. As a believer, whether you marry a Gospel worker or not, be very honest with your answers during a proposal interview. Don't pretend a spirituality that you don't live, and don't give the impression that you are willing to go to a pioneer field far from your relatives, when in your heart you know you never would want to go. To give the wrong impression will only complicate your own life as well as your husband's.

If you are a young man and God has called you to a tribal area, a pioneer field in North India or to a traveling ministry, explain honestly to your future wife the cost involved in being married to you. For example, she might have to leave her relatives, her village and home state, learn another language, eat strange food and accept possible suffering, poverty and persecution. If all you know is that God has called you to serve Him, help her understand clearly that she has to be willing to go with you wherever God sends you.

Of course, the person you consider marrying must have a personal walk with the Lord and a good report about his or her commitment and service from the pastor, other believers and neighbors. That walk has to be there independent of and *prior to* any proposal; otherwise, it might not last beyond the wedding day.

In the midst of all these decisions, let God's peace be your guide and rule your heart (Colossians 3:15). Make it your priority to seek His kingdom first.

EQUIPPED
FOR THE
Battle

6

WANTED
POSTER

*D*id you know that your picture is displayed on a wanted poster in hell?

Every time you succeed for Jesus, the price on your head goes up. If you belong to Jesus and your life has become in any way a threat to Satan's rule, you are known in hell!

Do you remember the story of the seven sons of Sceva in Acts 19? They were exorcists trying to free a man from an evil spirit. They themselves had never accepted Christ, but they tried to use His name for their mantra, hoping it would be the magic to cast out this devil. When the demon encountered them he said, "I recognize Jesus, and I know about Paul, but who are you?" (Acts 19:15).

The demon of course knew Jesus from eternity past, and also because of the defeat Satan suffered through the death and resurrection of the Son of God. He also knew Paul because he had seen his picture on the bulletin board in hell, and he had heard of his dangerous reputation.

When you study a wanted poster the police put up, you will find not only the picture of the criminal at large, but also his full name and a description that includes age, height, weight, hair color, eye color and other identification marks such as scars and birthmarks. Then of course there will be the charge, which can be anything from theft to assault to murder.

Hell has a name and a detailed description on your wanted poster as well. You have been studied carefully, and your weaknesses are written on your poster, so that whoever is assigned to attack you can zero in on your weak spots and not mistakenly on your strengths.

When we read and study the Bible about the devil and his demons, we realize that whole countries are under the authority of different demonic rulers. Each one seems to have a hierarchy of demon forces under him, assigned to oversee and rule various areas.

When you as a missionary step into a pioneer field, you must realize that your coming is a declaration of war. If there have never been any Christians before you, you also must realize that the demonic powers you encounter have never seen defeat before. Of course, Jesus overthrew Satan at the cross, and all of his demons know very well that one day their end will come. But try to imagine that these demons have been in authority over this country and this district since the fall of Adam, and possibly even since Lucifer and his demons were cast out of heaven. For thousands of years they have never had to move, given up their ground or even been challenged. As soon as people moved into these areas and built villages, these powers of darkness enslaved them as well.

In other countries and areas where true Christianity came hundreds of years ago, the demonic rulers of these places have had to move and relocate many times. Every time revival took place, they had to retreat. They know defeat from experience.

But you are now standing on the ground of a pioneer field where you will be the first one to challenge them in the name of Jesus. They are not used to this, and they have never tasted defeat in their own domain before. Please know that the devil will not give up any inch of his ground without a battle. And because you carry the name of Jesus to this village, you are the target.

I am not writing all this to scare you or to make you think more about the devil than is necessary. But I truly desire that you be aware of the reality of the warfare in the spirit world, so that you will keep on the alert and be prepared.

Perhaps you wonder why we still have to fight such difficult warfare when Satan was already defeated at Calvary. Why do we have to be so careful how we fight this battle? As children of God, are we not invincible? As heirs to the throne, are we not destined for victory? Do we not have the weapons of warfare and the power of the Spirit? And did not Jesus promise to be with us always? Yes, all this is true and more.

However, the realities of a final victory and the presence of Jesus with us do not eliminate the battle!

Our situation is the same as in the Old Testament when Joshua and the children of Israel were about to cross the Jordan River to enter the land of Canaan. The land was promised by God Himself to Abraham and to all his descendants. God confirmed His promise to the very generation that would actually set foot on the land to take possession of it. He even gave Joshua this tremendous promise:

> Moses My servant is dead; now therefore arise, cross this Jordan, you and all this people, to the land which I am giving to them, to the sons of Israel. Every place on which the sole of your foot treads, I have given it to you, just as I spoke to Moses. From the wilderness and this Lebanon, even as far as the great river, the river Euphrates, all the land of the Hittites, and as far as the Great Sea toward the setting of the sun, will be your territory.

No man will be able to stand before you all the days of
your life. Just as I have been with Moses, I will be with you;
I will not fail you or forsake you. Be strong and courageous,
for you shall give this people possession of the land which I
swore to their fathers to give them (Joshua 1:2-6).

But as you know from the story, the occupants of the land
did not drop dead or surrender the moment the children of
Israel crossed the Jordan River. They had to fight for every piece
of ground. God's presence was with them, the promise was
there, the victory was declared in the heavens; but they still had
to take the land step by step, driving out the enemy from each
town, each village and each corner of their land.

For 2,000 years now the victory has been ours, yet the territory remains to be taken and this is our task.

By the way, God doesn't consider it to be a defeat if we face
persecution, suffering or even death while we drive out the enemy and take the land. In fact, the death and resurrection of
Jesus won the greatest victory ever, and the blood of many martyrs that have gone before us caused the fastest growth of the
Church.

The devil takes your coming to this pioneer field very personally and very seriously. He will throw all his resources and all
his past experience into the fight, hoping to gain one more day,
one more week or one more year before he has to move.

Your invasion of his territory is for him a clear sign that the
coming of Jesus must be very, very near. He knows that if he
can drive you off, silence you or eliminate you altogether, he has
gained a little more time.

He knows very well that as long as you walk in humility and
obedience, totally depending on Jesus and in the power of the
Holy Spirit, he has no chance at all to overcome you, for you
will be truly invincible. Therefore, he has carefully studied your

weaknesses to find a way to trip you up and then to finish you off completely.

Jesus knows that in our own strength and with our own wisdom we are no match for the devil, regardless of how educated and experienced we might be. This is why Jesus told His disciples to watch and pray (Matthew 26:41) and to keep on the alert at all times (Luke 21:36).

Paul realized that the moment we drop our guard and make even a tiny compromise, we provide a crack in the door for Satan to come in and wound us. Because of this, Paul warned the believers in Romans 13:14, "But put on the Lord Jesus Christ, and make no provision for the flesh in regard to its lusts." With this verse Paul means that we ourselves are responsible to make no provision, that is, to give no chance and no opportunity for the flesh in regard to its lusts.

The flesh represents my old unsaved nature, which is totally selfish, rebellious, undisciplined and unwilling to obey God. Its lusts are the lures and ways of fulfilling the desires of this nature, which manifests itself in greed, envy, pride, immorality, self-gratification at the expense of others, anger and so on.

Along the way, when you find yourself and your ministry suddenly affected by any of these symptoms, Paul declares that this does not happen to you by chance. According to Romans 13:14, somewhere in the past you gave a little room, a little secret thought to the flesh.

Do you remember when you felt jealous that your co-worker was honored above you by your leader? Do you remember when you pretended you were glad that this other brother got a vehicle and some extra money for his ministry? Do you remember when you allowed pride to take over, and you felt others should have given you more honor and respect for your position? All these were only thoughts and feelings not followed by drastic outward actions, and you entertained them only for a few brief moments or days before you laid them aside. You considered them not important enough to ask forgiveness or to confess them to the Lord to receive His cleansing. However, hell noticed and made a record of it on your wanted poster. These very incidents become the weak spots that give the enemy the opportunity, a few months or years later, to be successful in an attack on you.

Our responsibility to prevent this from happening is twofold:

First of all, we must walk in the light and immediately receive cleansing and forgiveness for even what seem to be insignificant failures and sins.

Second, the Bible instructs us that we must *put on* the Lord Jesus Christ. This means that I must consciously and deliberately put Him on like clothing, until all of me is covered by all of Him. This is how I will look:

> *His mind* becomes mine and I will think the way He thinks. "Let this mind be in you, which was also in Christ Jesus" (Philippians 2:5, KJV).

> *His eyes* become mine and they see what He sees. "Behold, I say to you, lift up your eyes, and look on the fields, that they are white for harvest" (John 4:35).

> *His ears* become mine and they hear what the Father speaks. "And the things which I heard from Him, these I speak to the world" (John 8:26).

> *His hands, His feet, His mouth* will become mine and they will all cooperate to go, to preach and to bring freedom, deliverance and healing to others. "And as you go, preach, saying, 'The kingdom of heaven is at hand.' Heal the sick, raise the dead, cleanse the lepers, cast out demons; freely

you received, freely give" (Matthew 10:7-8). "And He said to them, 'Go into all the world and preach the gospel to all creation' " (Mark 16:15).

› *His will* becomes mine and I desire nothing that He would not want. "My food is to do the will of Him who sent Me, and to accomplish His work" (John 4:34).

› *His heart*, with His kindness, love and compassion, will become mine. "This is My commandment, that you love one another, just as I have loved you" (John 15:12).

› *His servanthood* will become the way I serve. "If I then, the Lord and the Teacher, washed your feet, you also ought to wash one another's feet" (John 13:14). "It is not so among you, but whoever wishes to become great among you shall be your servant, and whoever wishes to be first among you shall be your slave; just as the Son of Man did not come to be served, but to serve, and to give His life a ransom for many" (Matthew 20:26-28).

› *His humility and gentleness* will become part of my character. "Take My yoke upon you, and learn from Me, for I am gentle and humble in heart; and you shall find rest for your souls" (Matthew 11:29).

It all starts with my deliberate decision to put on Jesus instead of making room for my flesh to have its own way. The Bible tells us that our flesh must be crucified: "Now those who belong to Christ Jesus have crucified the flesh with its passions and desires" (Galatians 5:24).

Never expect this to happen automatically! My flesh does not crucify itself. I must do it. The Holy Spirit will direct and help me—but only as far as I am willing to go. Without crucifying the flesh, there is no way to put on Jesus. It is either one or the other.

If I put on Jesus to cover every part of my being, the devil will not find a single weak point, because now through Jesus my weakness has become my strength (2 Corinthians 12:10).

Remember, as long as you are a hindrance to Satan's kingdom, you will remain on his "most wanted" list.

7

GREAT AND
MIGHTY THINGS

A few years ago, a sensational story spread like wildfire all over Kerala and other parts of India.

A chemist had successfully blended some herbs together and in the process discovered a hair tonic that he proclaimed as the miracle cure for hair loss and baldness. The newspapers published pictures of people who testified about the amazing results they experienced after using this product.

The response was astonishing. People stood in lines several kilometers long to get a bottle of this secret hair tonic formula for themselves. Months later, the real truth came out: The hair tonic was a fake. It never did what its manufacturer claimed it would do.

I believe that we can get a lot of people interested and excited if we promise to reveal a hidden secret or mystery to them.

Do you know that God challenges us that if we call to Him, He too will tell us mysteries? Jeremiah 33:3 says, "Call to Me, and I will answer you, and I will tell you great and mighty things, which you do not know."

God spoke these words to Jeremiah the prophet just before the destruction of Jerusalem by Nebuchadnezzar's army. He couldn't have spoken it into a more desperate situation. The Chaldeans were besieging the city, and the prophet was in custody of the guard by order of the king. Jeremiah's message had been rejected. He was accused of being a collaborator with the enemy because he had foretold that Jerusalem would fall and be burned with fire.

To Jeremiah it must have looked like there would be nothing left of Israel and Judah after the Chaldeans were finished. But God had great and mighty plans in mind that would come to pass in the future, and He was ready to share them with Jeremiah and anyone else who cared to hear them.

At that moment in Jeremiah's ministry, nothing looked great and mighty: no miracles, no deliverance, no converts! All he could see were destruction and chaos. Yet God spoke about great and mighty things that Jeremiah couldn't even begin to imagine. God revealed to His prophet that He would have mercy, that He would restore the land and His people, and that once again there would be joy and peace.

Do you know that when Jesus looked at Peter, He saw great and mighty things that Peter couldn't see about himself? Peter saw himself sinking in the water, speaking up at the wrong times, making promises he couldn't keep and denying Jesus.

But Jesus saw an apostle who would stand up boldly to proclaim the Gospel, lead the Church, be the first one to take the Gospel to the heathen and be faithful until death.

I believe there are many secrets that God has that we know very little or nothing about. For instance, how can we understand all the events in the book of Revelation or know everything about the universe, the angels, God Himself or eternity?

However, there is one mystery that the believers of Old Testament times didn't know about at all, or perhaps had only a glimpse of it in prophecies but couldn't understand its meaning. This mystery is something great and mighty, and it is about us!

Perhaps you think, "There is surely nothing great and mighty about me—at least I can't see anything." Maybe you are like these Old Testament believers, and you haven't discovered it—yet.

Knowing this mystery is very important for our lives and especially for our ministries. However, if we don't know about it, it will not benefit us at all. We will be like a beggar who has a bank account in his name with 1 million rupees in it, but no one has told him. He remains a beggar in spite of all the wealth that rightfully could be at his disposal.

Our Christian lives, as well as our service to the Lord, will be weak, discouraging and often without much fruit if we aren't aware of these great and mighty things about ourselves. God is eager and willing to tell us this mystery, under one condition: if we call.

THE GREATEST MYSTERY AND THE MIGHTIEST THING—ABOUT ME

Paul wrote in a number of his letters about the mystery God has revealed to His people in the New Testament. It is the mightiest thing that can ever happen to a person:

> . . . that is, *the mystery* which has been hidden from the past ages and generations; but has now been manifested to His saints, to whom God willed to make known what is the riches of the glory of this mystery among the Gentiles, which is *Christ in you, the hope of glory* (Colossians 1:26–27).

> Do you not know that you are a temple of God, and that the Spirit of God dwells in you? (1 Corinthians 3:16).

> I have been crucified with Christ; and it is no longer I who live, but Christ lives in me (Galatians 2:20).

> But we have this treasure in earthen vessels, that the surpassing greatness of the power may be of God and not from ourselves (2 Corinthians 4:7).

In times past, even the greatest of saints could not imagine in their wildest dreams that the God of the universe would actually come and indwell every New Testament believer. Just think about the revelation of God that the Old Testament believers had:

Adam and Eve knew God more closely than anyone after them. They sinned once, and it cost them their relationship with Him and living in paradise. It earned them hard work, suffering and death not only for themselves but also for all the generations to come. An angel with a flaming sword stood guard at the entrance of their lost paradise, never allowing them to go back in.

Noah knew God as the One who destroyed every living thing that was not in the ark.

Abraham knew God as One who kept His promise but at the same time required a level of commitment, faith and obedience that made him an alien in a foreign land and caused him to be willing to sacrifice his only son.

The children of Israel saw God bringing great judgment over Pharaoh and all of Egypt and, in the end, drowning the entire Egyptian army in the Red Sea. Their revelation of God gave them an understanding that He was loving and merciful, provided for their needs, and delivered and protected them from their enemies—as long as they kept all His rules and didn't do anything to provoke Him.

At the same time, it was one of their most frightening experiences just to stand in His presence and listen to His voice. The mountain quaked violently; there were flashes of lightning and thunder, thick smoke, a loud trumpet and then a voice that scared them to death. Whenever they broke one of God's laws, death would follow. All this caused them to worship their God with fear and trembling.

Of course, many of the Old Testament believers had a closer relationship with God than most:

Enoch walked with God and was taken up.

Abraham was God's friend.

Moses spoke to Him face-to-face.

David was a man after God's own heart.

Elijah experienced mighty miracles in his ministry.

Daniel received amazing visions and revelations.

The Spirit of God came on some of these saints and prophets in a mighty way—but definitely not on every one in Israel. This doesn't mean that these believers in Jehovah did not love their God. They did—but with fear and trembling, and at a distance.

The Old Testament prophets, of course, foretold that one day God would pour out His Spirit over all flesh, change hearts of stone into hearts of flesh and cause people to seek the true and living God.

The interpretation of such prophecies must have been that one day true revival would come to Israel and people would turn to Jehovah, which would of course result in true worship and righteousness in their land. They would not have been able to imagine that the same God who answers by fire would actually come to live in the heart of a New Testament believer.

They would have trembled with fear at such a prospect and expected that this believer would live a very short life. One wrong thought, one wrong word, and the holy and righteous God would surely strike that person dead.

Only in Jesus did we receive the complete revelation of God. We discovered that our God is not only holy and righteous, but He is also merciful, compassionate and full of love. In fact, the Bible says that He is love. This love found a way to make us righteous by sacrificing Himself as a payment for our sin. Because He Himself died for us, we were able to become a clean temple for God to indwell us.

Without this revelation, I believe that no one would have dared to ask Jesus into his heart. But now, we have this treasure—Jesus—in an earthen vessel—us! The Spirit of God has come to dwell in us permanently, never to leave us. Truly Christ in us, the hope of glory, is the greatest and mightiest thing God could have ever planned for our lives here on earth.

It has suddenly become possible to know Him and the power of His resurrection, not from afar but very closely. You see, I do not live any longer, but Christ lives in me and through me.

The mystery about us is this: We, as believers, contain the mightiest power of the universe—God Himself (Christ in us). We, the container or vessel, might not look impressive at all, but it's what's in us that counts!

Our son Daniel likes firecrackers. Some of them look so small and innocent. But wait until he lights them! They are "dynamite"! You see, the packaging is not what's important, but the content.

We are a walking package of God's dynamite. We are the wrapper and Jesus is the dynamite. Actually, the comparison with a firecracker is too weak, because the firecracker and the powder in it are usable only one time. Jesus in us is a permanent, self-charging dynamite that never loses its power and is always ready to explode and make an impact!

Do you know what this revelation that Paul talks about means for your life and your ministry? It actually means that because of Jesus in you, there are no limits for God to work through your life!

› With Christ in you, all things are possible.

› He is able to win every battle.

> There are no limits to His power.

> In Him, you have all you ever need.

> Because of Him living in you, you are a new creation; you are an overcomer and you are permitted to come boldly to the throne of grace.

Can you recognize this mystery? Can you see it and live it? Dear brother, dear sister, if you do not understand this mystery in your life and ministry, you will always limit God.

Our Spirit Must Know It

Perhaps you knew all these mighty things long ago, and you have read them a thousand times, but they never did anything for you. Perhaps the problem is that your head knows it, but your spirit doesn't know it yet, and therefore you cannot live by it.

God told Jeremiah to call to Him so He could in turn tell him these wonderful things that he didn't know or couldn't even imagine in his present condition. God was able to speak to Jeremiah in such a way that the words he heard were not just in Jeremiah's head or on a scroll, but they went deep into his heart, or spirit. They became such a powerful part of his life that Jeremiah was able to believe them, proclaim them, look for their fulfillment and live by these promises of God.

In the very same way, we must ask God to speak these mighty things to our spirits so we can live by them. Unless they are in our spirit, all these great things are useless to us, because we are not able to apply them.

But how do we get God's message from our heads to our hearts, or spirits? The secret is this: *Call to Him.* When God speaks, He *never* speaks to the head—He always speaks to the heart. He has given us this promise: "I *will* tell you." This means, "I will tell your spirit."

I remember a night when I was troubled about a need I had. In fact, I felt sad and discouraged, and I couldn't sleep. I knew God's promises, but they seemed so far away and my need was so real.

I got up from my bed, took my Bible and went into the kitchen. My desire was for God to speak His promises into my heart so they could become real to me. After I sat down at the table, I opened my Bible to read Matthew 6:31–32:

> Do not be anxious then, saying, "What shall we eat?" or "What shall we drink?" or "With what shall we clothe ourselves?" For all these things the Gentiles eagerly seek; for your heavenly Father knows that you need all these things.

I underlined "Do not be anxious . . . for your heavenly Father knows that you need all these things." For me, it was so important that God knew my need, that He was aware of it. However, the words seemed to be just on the paper, but not in my spirit.

I began to read this one sentence over and over to myself for several hours. As I did this, I began to realize that slowly some of the words had started to penetrate my heart. I kept reading until my spirit got the message: "Don't be anxious—for your heavenly Father knows."

Do you know what happened when my spirit was able to grasp this truth? It created faith. And faith can already see God's answer before it happens. Instead of tears and an anxious heart, I went to bed with real joy and peace, *knowing* beyond the shadow of a doubt that my Father knew my need and that He would meet it.

Call to the Lord and ask Him to speak into your spirit what it truly means that Christ is living in you.

8

YOU ARE NO
SURPRISE TO GOD

God's call is on your life. You have just finished Bible school, and you are excited and ready to launch out.

Yesterday you heard your Bible school principal give the farewell message at your graduation. At the end of the service, you and the others knelt down before the Lord to dedicate your lives to take the Gospel of Jesus Christ to the unreached villages of your country.

Today you boarded a train that will take you to a pioneer field you have never seen before and to a people who not only speak a different language, but whose lifestyle and customs are almost opposite to your own.

As you travel along, you wonder if you will be able to learn their language, eat their food, win their trust and plant a church. Yesterday everything looked so exciting, but today fear grips your heart, especially when you consider your own abilities and qualifications. Again and again you ask yourself: "What happens if God's call and plan are too much and too high for me to accomplish?"

> > > > >

Perhaps you have already worked for the past five years in a district of Bihar. You know without a doubt that God has called you to this place. But nothing much seems to happen. You've fasted, you've prayed, you've preached, you've witnessed; but the fruit seems so meager: a handful of believers scattered over several villages. God specifically told you to establish a church in each of the 27 villages of this district. But after all your efforts, there is only one small gathering of about eight believers.

You look back over the past five years, and you ask yourself with fear and trembling, "Did I fail? Was the call too high for me? Do I lack the abilities it takes to do the job? Should God have called someone else to do this work—someone with more education, more experience and more power?"

> > > > >

Perhaps you have already established a good work in a pioneer field. But two months ago, you made some foolish decisions that caused several of your co-workers to leave. At the time, you considered the welfare of your family, but you forgot to evaluate how your co-workers might feel. When you saw the damaging effects of your choice, you immediately called for a meeting, reversed your decision and asked your co-workers for forgiveness.

Right now it seems as though the problem has been solved, and peace returned within the team. However, you feel humiliated, and you are angry with yourself for having made such a mistake. You should have known better, especially since God has entrusted you with the leadership of this work. Now you have doubts if you really have what it takes to oversee this pioneer work and to be the example of a leader that your co-workers need.

> > > > >

I believe there will be times in our service for the Lord when each of us comes to a place where we wonder whether God's call is too much to accomplish, and we fear that we cannot do it. I have found a passage in the New Testament that deals with this issue. It has encouraged me many times when I wonder whether I am the right person for the job I am called to do:

> Now great multitudes were going along with Him; and He turned and said to them, "If anyone comes to Me, and does not hate his own father and mother and wife and children and brothers and sisters, yes, and even his own life, he cannot be My disciple. Whoever does not carry his own cross and come after Me cannot be My disciple.
>
> "For which one of you, when he wants to build a tower, does not first sit down and calculate the cost, to see if he has enough to complete it? Otherwise, when he has laid a foundation, and is not able to finish, all who observe it begin to ridicule him, saying, 'This man began to build and was not able to finish.'
>
> "Or what king, when he sets out to meet another king in battle, will not first sit down and take counsel whether he is strong enough with ten thousand men to encounter the one coming against him with twenty thousand? Or else, while the other is still far away, he sends a delegation and asks terms of peace. So therefore, no one of you can be My disciple who does not give up all his own possessions" (Luke 14:25-33).

When Jesus spoke to the multitude that had gathered around Him, He clearly outlined the cost of discipleship and how His potential followers should go about making the decision whether or not to follow Him.

Much of the crowd was there because of the great miracles He performed. Never had they seen anyone who could multiply bread to feed 5,000, heal the lepers, open blind eyes, raise the dead and cast out demons. His teaching was wonderful and distinctly different from their religious leaders. He spoke with authority yet with such love that God seemed very near to them. Sometimes some of these scribes or Pharisees would show up to debate Him or to ask trick questions. Wherever Jesus showed up, there was excitement, and people were eager to get in on the action!

Jesus was able to discern the mixed motives of the crowd, as well as the true hunger for the living God that some of the people had. He loved them all, but He knew He could never build God's kingdom with people who followed Him blindly, unaware of the price tag of discipleship.

You see, Jesus clearly saw the cross ahead of Him and His followers, down through the centuries to come. To truly become His disciple, each person had to make a conscious, careful and deliberate decision that would last a lifetime—one that included no thought of turning back, however heated the battle might become.

Jesus illustrated the seriousness of such a decision in Luke 14:28-31:

> For which one of you, when he wants to build a tower, does not first sit down and calculate the cost, to see if he has enough to complete it? Otherwise, when he has laid a foundation, and is not able to finish, all who observe it begin to ridicule him, saying, "This man began to build and was not able to finish."
>
> Or what king, when he sets out to meet another king in battle, will not first sit down and take counsel whether he is strong enough with ten thousand men to encounter the one coming against him with twenty thousand?

Jesus told about a man who wanted to build a tower. The first step he took was not to go out to buy material, hire workers or lay the foundation stone. Jesus said that before this man ever started building anything, the most logical, normal and absolutely necessary step was to sit down, evaluate the whole building project, calculate the expense and figure out if he has enough money to be able to complete the job.

To further explain and clarify His point, Jesus told the crowd that there is no king anywhere who would be so foolish as to go into battle without first sitting down and evaluating the strength of his army in comparison to the army of the enemy. Based on his careful investigation, the king would then make his decision whether to go to war or not.

From these two stories, we can easily see that Jesus has no intention at all of tricking anyone into joining His army by covering up the cost. I believe that we also have the responsibility to ourselves, and to the rest of the Body of Christ, to clearly understand and present the terms of discipleship. In this way, every one of us can make up his or her mind as to how far and how deep we want to go in our commitment to Christ. However, in order for Jesus to build His Church, He needs more than just a crowd of spectators and more than just merely believers. He needs disciples.

This passage of Scripture not only helps us make vital decisions regarding our Christian walk, but it reveals something very, very important about our God and about His call for us to serve Him. You see, when Jesus counseled people, He didn't just pass out good neighborly advice or solve their problems with superior intelligence or knowledge of human psychology.

Whenever we read any of His spoken words, we must remember that Jesus Himself is *the* Way, *the* Truth and *the* Life. He is *the* Wisdom of God. Therefore, whatever truth He spoke was not human wisdom, but the eternal words and revelations of God. Whatever Jesus proclaimed and commanded us to do here on earth was exactly what He had seen being the *normal practice*

in heaven. This is why His words and actions were so revolutionary, so offensive and so out of this world. For example:

> Love your enemies, and pray for those who persecute you
> (Matthew 5:44).
>
> Do not be anxious for tomorrow (Matthew 6:34).
>
> But the greatest among you shall be your servant (Matthew
> 23:11).

Do you remember the prayer He taught His disciples? One
of the lines in it goes like this: "Thy will be done, on earth *as it
is in heaven*" (Matthew 6:10).

For Jesus, there was no doubt that the right and only ac-
ceptable ways of worship, relationship and life altogether were
how all these were already done in heaven. Therefore, He lived
according to heaven's rules and heaven's example. He wanted
all His followers to adopt and implement "the heavenly way of
doing things" right here on earth in their everyday life and in
their service to Him.

In this Scripture from Luke, Jesus explains to the crowd
what the right way would be for this builder, this king and this
potential disciple to arrive at an appropriate decision regarding
the tasks ahead of them. Between the lines, Jesus actually says
this: "In order to make these endeavors successful, this is the
way heaven would handle it."

In the light of all this, I believe that the illustrations of the
man who wants to build a tower as well as the king who plans to
go to war are also illustrations of our God Himself.

As the King of kings, His goal is to build His kingdom in
places where His name is not known and where Satan's throne
has been until now. This means that He is planning to invade
enemy territory. It is absolutely certain that it will be a fierce
struggle, probably with many battles. Satan will not give up his

rule easily. He will command the powers of darkness to march against the army of God and to attack it with the goal of destroying these invading forces.

Jesus said that *no* king will blindly go into a battle. Please know that our King follows His own advice as well.

What does this mean for you? *Before* God ever called you to join His army in Nepal or India or China, He sat down to carefully evaluate whether He could go to battle with you as a soldier in His army and whether He could win the battle by sending you to the front lines.

Dear brother, dear sister, please know this: You are no surprise to God! You might be amazed by your failures, your lack of courage and your struggle with faithfulness, but God is not! He knew exactly what He would have on His hands when He called you.

Please read Psalm 139. It tells you how much and how intimately God knows you. He knows your innermost thoughts, your fears and your failures, both now and those of the future. He is aware of your frame and that you are made of dust.

Just like this king in the story that Jesus told, before you were called to serve God, He made a complete inventory of you. Everything you are and everything you are not—He figured all of it into His calculation.

His inventory and careful evaluation revealed that you could not do the job.

He cannot win India with you in His army, nor can He defeat the powers of darkness in that village where he intended to station you. Your resources of strength, endurance and power are insufficient and inferior to those of the enemy. In your present condition, it would be impossible for you to succeed. This is how God's evaluation paper reads:

Peter is too impulsive.

Thomas does not have enough faith and doubts everything.
John sleeps when he is supposed to pray.
James has the same problem.
Mary Magdalene looks for a dead Messiah, even after Jesus foretold His resurrection.

_____ (put your name here) doesn't have the stuff it takes to qualify as a soldier.

A MAJOR ADJUSTMENT

When God looked at us as potential recruits for His army and then evaluated the forces of the enemy, He knew right away that He would lose the war unless He made a major adjustment within His people . . . and He did! He decreed: "I will put My Spirit within you" (Ezekiel 36:27), and "You shall receive power" (Acts 1:8).

This means that when you accepted Jesus, you became a child of God. Jesus is now living in you through the Holy Spirit. This entitles you to all that God has promised in His Word, including the promise that you will receive power. God wants to release the power of His Holy Spirit into your life, just as He empowered Jesus and the apostles. God's purpose for this is to qualify you for battle. As you go in the power of the Holy Spirit, not in your own, you will be able to defeat the enemy and, with His power, fulfill God's plan for your life.

God says that each of us will receive this power as a gift *freely* given from Him, just by asking in faith.

Here are a few Bible verses that will help you understand the kind of power it is that God wants you to have in your ministry. They will show you just what the Holy Spirit and His power could do in your service to the Lord.

> God has not given us a spirit of timidity [fear], *but of power and love and discipline* (2 Timothy 1:7).

But you shall receive power when the Holy Spirit has come upon you; and *you shall be My witnesses* both in Jerusalem, and in all Judea and Samaria, and even to the remotest part of the earth (Acts 1:8).

And they were all filled with the Holy Spirit, and began to *speak the word* of God *with boldness* (Acts 4:31).

But He who is coming after me is mightier than I. . . . He Himself [Jesus] will baptize you with the *Holy Spirit and fire* (Matthew 3:11).

Now we have received, not the spirit of the world, but the Spirit who is from God, *that we might know the things freely given to us by God* (1 Corinthians 2:12).

And I will ask the Father, and He will give you another *Helper, that He may be with you forever*; that is the Spirit of truth . . . but you know Him because *He abides with you*, and will be in you (John 14:16–17).

But the Helper [Comforter], the Holy Spirit, whom the Father will send in My name, *He will teach you all things*, and bring to your remembrance all that I said to you (John 14:26).

But when He, the Spirit of truth, comes, *He will guide you into all the truth* (John 16:13).

And when they arrest you and deliver you up, do not be anxious beforehand about what you are to say, but say whatever is given you in that hour; *for it is not you who speak, but it is the Holy Spirit* (Mark 13:11).

The love of God has been poured out within our hearts through the Holy Spirit who was given to us (Romans 5:5).

That you may *abound in hope by the power of the Holy Spirit* (Romans 15:13).

Guard, through the Holy Spirit who dwells in us, *the treasure* which has been entrusted to you (2 Timothy 1:14).

And *renewing by the Holy Spirit,* whom He poured out upon us richly through Jesus Christ our Savior (Titus 3:5-6).

Make an honest survey of your personal life and ministry, and check if you lack any of these things:

> › *Power* to confront and drive out the powers of darkness that hold people's lives and whole nations in bondage
>
> › *Love* for the people of your mission field and for your enemies
>
> › *Discipline* in your personal life, ministry, outreach, study of God's Word and prayer
>
> › *Hope* for your lost relatives, for your needs to be met and for souls to be saved
>
> › *Ability and boldness* to witness and to fearlessly proclaim God's Word
>
> › A *burning fire in your heart,* instead of coldness and indifference, to reach the lost, to love Jesus more than the whole world and to be willing to lay down your life for the Gospel
>
> › *Understanding* with your heart, not with your head, who you are in Christ and what God gave you freely in Jesus
>
> › *Someone to help you and stay with you always,* even if others reject or leave you, or if there are no believers yet on your mission field with whom you could have fellowship
>
> › *Comfort* in times of suffering, loneliness and failure
>
> › *Teaching and guidance* in understanding and applying Scripture
>
> › *Advice* for what to say and how to behave during times of persecution and interrogation
>
> › *Someone who helps you guard* your walk with the Lord, your

ministry, your message and your gifts entrusted to you

> *Renewal* when you are weary, tired and discouraged

If you lack any of these things, the Holy Spirit and His power are the solution to your problems!

The power God desires to release in our lives is not for any of our own selfish purposes, but to qualify us for warfare against the powers of darkness. With it we will not only be better witnesses, but as God has calculated it—we will win the war.

He now declares, "The tower can be built; the war can be won; India, China, Myanmar and the world will know Jesus— through your life empowered by My Holy Spirit."

It is very important for you to allow the Holy Spirit to take over every area of your life and to release His power to conquer every struggle, every fear and every doubt. When you see mountains before you, when you doubt your abilities, when the task given to you seems too difficult, when the pressure becomes too much, when you have failed—remind yourself of this: "I am no surprise to God. My God counted the cost before He called me. He found it sufficient to win the battle using my life, because He has filled me with His Spirit."

HIS
Ambassadors

9

SENT AS
JESUS WAS

*I*ndia is full of surprises, especially where the climate is concerned. More than once I have found myself unprepared when I've traveled around in the country.

This time I had come to a small village, and I stayed with some local believers. During the daytime it had been quite warm, but I discovered that the nights were much colder than I ever expected. I had no blanket to cover me, and everyone in the house was already asleep.

In the morning, I was supposed to speak at a ladies' meeting. After all my traveling, I wanted to get some rest. I pulled an extra sari and skirt out of my travel bag and laid them on top of me, but the clothes were too slippery, and every time I turned, they fell off.

After an hour of useless attempts to get some sleep, I felt frustrated and discouraged. "I wish the people who invited me to come would have taken better care of me," I thought. "They should have known how cold it is here at night. They could have at least provided a blanket." I felt quite dissatisfied with their care for me.

All of a sudden, the Lord interrupted my thoughts; He asked me, "Why did you come here?" He didn't wait for my reply but gave the answer Himself: "You came to serve, not to be served."

That was all He said, but it was so convicting that I was able to immediately and clearly recognize the wrong attitude in my heart. I was so shook up with my discovery that I switched on my flashlight and wrote these words on a piece of paper: "I came to serve, not to be served." The Lord had reminded me of something so important that I wanted to make sure I didn't forget it. For a long time that night, I thought about the meaning of this verse from Matthew 20:28, before I finally fell asleep.

In John 20:21, Jesus told His disciples, "As the Father has sent Me, I also send you." According to this verse, we are sent to this world and especially to the people of our mission field, just like Jesus was sent by the Father. This means that we are expected by God Himself to speak, act and live exactly as Jesus would do, displaying His attitudes, His values and His expectations.

Let us look at a few of these characteristics that Jesus displayed.

TO SERVE, NOT TO BE SERVED

In Matthew 20:26–28, Jesus laid down His revolutionary strategy for the building of His kingdom and its function once it was established:

> Whoever wishes to become great among you shall be your servant, and whoever wishes to be first among you shall be your slave; just as the Son of Man did not come to be served, but to serve, and to give His life a ransom for many.

I don't know what the disciples thought when they first heard Jesus' idea, but I am quite sure it blew them away. What

Jesus was trying to implement was so diametrically opposed to any example of authority—political or religious—that they had ever encountered. I am certain they must have almost panicked at the thought of how this would look practically and even if it could be done altogether.

Jesus had the answer for them in verse 28. He said, "The Son of Man did not come to be served, but to serve." In other words, He told them, "Just watch Me and do as I do, and the end result will line up with My strategy."

Do you know why I felt discouraged and frustrated that night when I didn't have a blanket? It was because I had come with expectations of what others should do for me. I felt bad because my expectations weren't met.

Jesus, on the contrary, came with only one desire and goal: to serve others. If they didn't do anything for Him, He wasn't disappointed, because He came to them without a preconceived plan as to how they should meet His needs.

When you go to a village to evangelize or when you are invited to speak in a church, what secret expectations do you have? If you wait for people to give you a special welcome, provide nice food and accommodations, serve your every need and take care of you, you are liable to get your feelings hurt.

It is much safer to come with the attitude of Jesus: "I came to serve, not to be served." Then, if people reject us or don't treat us "first class," our love toward them is free to remain the same. We can't be disappointed because there will be no unfulfilled expectations.

To Give, Not to Receive

If there is anything that characterizes our God, it is His giving nature. He gave us our very lives, our health, our families, food, clothing, shelter, sunshine, rain and everything else we need on this earth. Then He gave us His ultimate gift: Jesus. In

Him is wrapped up all that heaven has to offer: peace, joy, truth, light, wisdom, love, forgiveness, freedom, deliverance, eternal life, healing, access to God, the right to become children of God—and my list could go on. With Jesus, God has withheld nothing from us.

When Jesus walked this earth, He gave sight to the blind, healing to the sick, restoration to the lepers, freedom to those bound by Satan and the Gospel to the spiritually poor and hungry. He gave His time, His strength, His comfort and His compassion to all who came to Him.

He did all this freely—without an outstretched hand that was waiting for payment. He gave of Himself, His power and His love, without first checking if it would bring Him some benefits or at least some extra honor from the council in Jerusalem.

His giving was not calculated. He actually went out, searching everywhere for people who would like to accept His free gift. In John 7:37 we read, "Now on the last day, the great day of the feast, Jesus stood and cried out, saying, 'If any man is thirsty, let him come to Me and drink.' "

What did it mean practically for Jesus to make such a public announcement? It meant that thousands of people with terrible problems would rush to Him and stay there, even if it took days, until He had helped them. By the time He had preached to them, answered their questions, healed their diseases, freed them from demon possession and listened to all their burdens and heartaches, He was totally exhausted and physically worn out. Then He would need to spend nights in prayer to His Father to prepare Himself spiritually for the next crowd.

He gave Himself freely to people who had nothing to give back to Him. He had come to give, not to receive. This was His attitude that He taught to His disciples before He sent them out for ministry: "As you go, preach, saying, 'The kingdom of heaven is at hand.' Heal the sick, raise the dead, cleanse the lepers, cast out demons; freely you received, freely give" (Matthew 10:7–8).

Paul reminded the believers in Acts 20:35, "Remember the words of the Lord Jesus, that He Himself said, 'It is more blessed to give than to receive.' "

What about us? If the Lord has equipped us with gifts, talents and a definite calling to do His ministry, what is our attitude on giving? I believe that our ability to freely give is often limited by the desire to make a profit and by greed. Here are some questions for you:

Do you expect money in return for coming to someone's house to pray for their sickness? Are you visiting those houses in the village more often where you know you will receive a nice meal and a gift of money every time you go there? If you preach and they give you a much smaller gift than what you expected, are you unhappy? I know of some evangelists who demand a certain amount of money guaranteed for their services; otherwise, they will not come at all.

Nowhere does Jesus say that we are not allowed to accept someone's gift or hospitality while we are about His business. On the contrary, He says in Luke 10:7, "Stay in that house, eating and drinking what they give you; for the laborer is worthy of his wages." And Paul wrote to the Galatians, "Let the one who is taught the word share all good things with him who teaches" (Galatians 6:6).

The Lord knows we have needs, and He expects the believers to take care of their pastor. However, for the protection of ourselves and our spiritual lives and for the reputation and purity of our ministries as well as the name of God, He wants us to be free from seeking gifts. He knows how fast it could turn into a mere business.

Jesus wants us to be able to minister freely to all who are in need of the living God. Our ministry must be as joyful, as dedicated and as loving whether we get something or nothing from those whom we serve.

If we come to our mission field to give what God has given to us with no expectations to receive anything in return, we act as Jesus would. Why not target homes of poor people in your community, where you know for sure that they have nothing to give, so that you can experience the joy of blessing others?

TO LOVE, NOT TO EXPECT LOVE

"For God so loved the world . . ." (John 3:16). When we read this verse, we immediately realize that God's love is absolutely different from ours.

Just imagine for a moment: God, holy and righteous, looks down from heaven to see a world in total chaos. People are killing each other, choosing to indulge in every sin they can find and serving the devil with every fiber of their being. God is actually looking at fallen creatures who defy Him and who hate Him and everything that is holy, and His reaction is not immediate destruction—but love. In fact, He loved them so much that He gave His only Son to die for them.

Jesus loved us, not after we straightened out, repented and just maybe deserved His mercy. No, He loved us while we were still sinners and God's enemies (Romans 5:8). When Jesus came to this world, He came to give us His love, regardless of whether we loved Him back or not.

All of us desire to be loved, and we search for someone or something that will meet this need. However, our human capability and understanding of love has definite limits. For us, love is a two-way street. I do nice things for you, and you respond by doing nice things for me. I meet some of your needs, and I expect you to meet some of mine. I show kindness and friendship, and you owe the same to me. If you don't follow this rule, then I look for someone else.

Perhaps our highest form of love is that of a mother for her own child. She has almost endless patience, time and effort to bring up this child. She might even lay down her life on behalf of the child if necessary. When the child is small, he responds with a smile, with joy to see his mother. Theirs is a very close relationship. However, this love is usually limited to a mother's own child. It will not easily transfer to just any child off of the street.

The love between a husband and wife has limits as well. The wife can only take so much ill-treatment or neglect until she starts to become incapable of loving her husband. A husband can only forgive to a certain point before his love dies away. Their relationship then becomes parallel living, with bitterness and conflict instead of love.

Jesus' love is on a far higher level, which is impossible for the world to achieve. His love has no limits, does not manipulate, bears all things, forgives all things and never fails. It is beyond this world and part of a different, divine nature. It is so strikingly different that Jesus proclaimed it to be the mark of recognition for His followers before the world: "By this all men will know that you are My disciples, if you have love for one another" (John 13:35).

This love cannot be duplicated. It cannot be produced by discipline, philosophy, religious exercise or any other means. It is the direct result of Christ Himself living in a believer's heart. His love flows out of the believer's life, and Christ is the source and supply of it.

The ability to love like Jesus loves puts all our human relationships on a higher level: We can love freely, even if we are not loved back. We become capable of not only loving a neighbor or stranger, but our enemies as well. With this love we are able to restore broken relationships, because our forgiveness goes beyond human limits.

When we come to our mission field with this kind of ability to love freely, we will not look for others to love us. This will be our most powerful weapon, and its impact on people who have never encountered the love of God before will be far greater than we can ever imagine.

TO MINISTER, NOT TO RECEIVE MINISTRY

As a believer, when you attend your church on Sunday, the weekly prayer meeting or an evangelistic crusade, what is your attitude? Do you come with the following expectation: "Today I hope to receive a special blessing from my pastor's sermon and some comfort and encouragement to help me go through my problems at work. I also expect the pastor to lay hands on me and pray for my healing because I have a sore throat."

➤ ➤ ➤ ➤ ➤

As a Bible school student, when you attend your classes and listen to your teachers, does this go through your mind: "I hope the class is good enough today to make my attendance worthwhile. I expect to hear something new and exciting that is useful when I have a chance to do some outreach work. I hope to succeed in developing a close relationship with my teachers and principal. This will help me get more chances to preach in some good meetings."

➤ ➤ ➤ ➤ ➤

As a pastor or evangelist, when you attend a conference with a special guest speaker, what are your thoughts and hopes as you come?

Do you come with the expectation that this famous speaker should take time to recognize you publicly, because you are quite important yourself? Are you waiting for a private audience so you might have a chance to develop some kind of friendship that would be profitable for your name and ministry? Perhaps you come expecting to see great miracles, receive new revelations, and through the ministry of this brother end up with new faith, new strength, greater vision and enthusiasm. Most of all, you hope that somehow a little of his anointing will rub off on you.

> > > > >

Is it all wrong to come to church, Bible school or a conference with expectations? No, of course not. If we don't expect something, then nothing will happen. But when you look a little closer at the things I listed, you will recognize that all these expectations are pretty self-centered: "I want to be healed, encouraged, blessed, anointed and so on. I want my pastor, teacher or elder to minister to me."

What happens if we don't get what we came for? What if the pastor preached a sermon that didn't teach me anything new? What if no one prayed for my need? What if the elders, the pastor and his wife were too busy counseling others and didn't have time to listen to my story? What if no one at church comforted me when I was sad, visited me when I was sick and encouraged me when I was down?

What if the Bible school teacher didn't consider me for the opportunity to preach?

What if the conference speaker didn't shake my hand because someone forgot to introduce me? What if others were blessed and ministered to, but the speaker had to leave to catch his train before he ever got the chance to pray for me and my need?

What is our reaction and how deeply are we disappointed when one of these things happens to us? Do we become bitter? Do we doubt God's love and care for us?

Perhaps you think or even say something like this: "This pastor, or this pastor's wife, doesn't care for me at all. I won't share my vegetable produce with them anymore because they can't even visit me when I am sick. Anyway, the old pastor we had before was better. It looks like no one loves me at church, and I am not going back for the next three weeks. Let them see if they can do all the church work without my help and expertise."

Jesus was different. Wherever He went, He looked for people who needed His ministry. Just think of Nicodemus, the woman at the well, the lepers, the children and His disciples. Jesus didn't ask them to minister to Him, bless Him, build Him up, encourage Him or pray for Him. He had come to minister to others, even if others never ministered to Him.

I believe that Jesus was in need of ministry; but only a few people, if any, recognized it.

There were some who helped meet the physical needs of Jesus and His disciples, and it surely was a blessing and help. Jesus had some friends, such as Lazarus and his sisters, who welcomed Him and His disciples into their home. Jesus surely enjoyed their friendship.

There were those who admired Him, talked about His miracles and invited Him for dinner.

Then there were His disciples and closest friends. They went with Him through many difficult situations and wonderful experiences as well. They walked with Him all around the country for three years, and they shared His life and ministry. I am certain that Jesus was glad for their fellowship, friendship and love.

But when it came to spiritual ministry, the disciples seemed to be always on the receiving end. We don't ever read that they went to Jesus to strengthen Him for His battles. Perhaps they didn't feel qualified to minister to Him in that way. However, most of the time when they tried to help Him out, they either misunderstood His purpose or ended up having personal problems.

Perhaps we have never considered that Jesus needed ministry. After all, He was the Son of God and was above everything and everyone else. Yet we forget that He laid down all His glory to become as human as we are. Throughout His ministry, He had to face temptations and attacks from Satan himself. At the end of His life was the cross and the most terrible battle the spirit world had ever seen.

I believe that if someone had offered to minister to Jesus, perhaps praying for Him, reading Scripture to Him and encouraging Him, He would have gladly accepted it. God the Father certainly believed that Jesus needed ministry. We read that, after His temptation in the wilderness "the devil left Him; and behold, angels came and began to minister to Him" (Matthew 4:11). And while Jesus struggled in prayer in Gethsemane, Luke 22:43 tells us, "Now an angel from heaven appeared to Him, strengthening Him."

What am I trying to say here? Rather than feeling sorry for ourselves when others have failed to minister to us, we must search for someone who needs our ministry.

Just think for a moment: How heavy are the burdens your pastor, your elders, and your pastor's wife carry? You only know a small fraction of them, because much will be very confidential. How many sheep are in their care? Do you know the agony it takes to bring just one Christian from his spiritual birth to maturity? Do you know how many nights they pray, fast and cry out to God on behalf of those He has entrusted into their care?

Do you know what it means for a pastor's family life if he and his wife are on call 24 hours a day, seven days a week, and that for the whole village? Besides all this, preaching and teaching take enormous strength out of the pastor, because they are not just lectures, but spiritual confrontations.

The Bible school teacher and the conference speaker face similar situations. Everyone expects them to minister to their needs. People look at them for answers, revelation, guidance, healing, miracles, leadership and anointing. Everyone assumes that their position puts them above normal difficulties, temptations and struggles. They are expected to be stronger than normal Christians.

Let me tell you, these people who teach and lead have a desperate need to be ministered to, because they are constantly giving of themselves and receiving so little from others. What they do receive is admiration, honor and recognition, none of which necessarily helps them in their struggle against pride.

The higher the level of their leadership, the more intense and critical will be their spiritual battles. The devil knows that if they fall, it will affect thousands of others as well. Have you ever considered ministering to them instead of expecting them to minister to you?

But you may wonder how you could possibly minister to one of them, especially because they are in a leadership position and you are not. Ministering does not always mean that you walk up to someone, lay your hands on their head and say a prayer or pronounce a blessing over them. It means that you seek every opportunity to be a blessing and a strength to them.

Give words of encouragement, of appreciation and of thanks. Pray diligently for them and with them if you have a close enough relationship. Be one with them in your heart. Support their efforts of evangelism, teaching and outreach with your attitude, words and participation.

When you go to church, go to Bible school or attend the conference, attend with a mind-set that is not self-centered. Come to minister to others and to be used by God to be an added strength to your pastor, your pastor's wife, your Bible school teacher or the conference speaker.

If you first seek to minister to others, God will be faithful to send others to you if you need ministry.

To Worship God in Order to Give to Him

So far we have considered how we should come to our mission field or to our church with the attitudes of Jesus: looking for opportunities to serve, to give, to love and to minister rather than expecting others to do these things to us.

Now I would like for us to look at one attitude that is considered to be very important throughout the Bible, one that has nothing to do with our neighbor, our pastor or our mission field—but with God Himself: to come to God for the sole purpose of blessing Him, ministering to Him and giving worship to Him, without looking for or calculating the benefits we might obtain.

Most of the time, when we approach God in our services with singing, prayers, testimonies and so on, we have a dual purpose in mind. One is to praise God. At the same time, we want to bless the people in the congregation, encourage them, help their faith grow and get them into a joyful mood that makes the rest of the service even more wonderful. It is the prelude to seeing miracles happen and people getting healed and saved. Most of our services are designed and set up to bring about these results.

Is there anything wrong with this? No—God Himself set up this very principle: Whatever we give to Him will result in blessing to ourselves. However, many of us have turned our worship to God into a self-centered business. We use worship and praise as a calculated means to get something for ourselves.

There is a higher level of worship that the Bible clearly talks about—it is for God's benefit, not for ours! It is ministering to God Himself. We come to Him in order to meet His needs.

It is easy for us to understand that we have needs, but to discover that God has needs as well sounds almost unbelievable, even frightening. There are a number of Bible verses that tell us the kind of worship and ministry we should give to our God. By examining the things we should give Him, we can then recognize what His needs are.

> *Love.* "And you shall love the LORD your God with all your heart and with all your soul and with all your might" (Deuteronomy 6:5).

> *Service.* "Serve the LORD with gladness" (Psalm 100:2).

> *Blessing.* "Bless the LORD, O my soul; and all that is within me, bless His holy name. Bless the LORD, O my soul, and forget none of His benefits" (Psalm 103:1–2).

> *Praise.* "Praise the LORD! Praise God in His sanctuary; praise Him in His mighty expanse. Praise Him for His mighty deeds." (Psalm 150:1–2).

> *Singing.* "Sing praise to the LORD, you His godly ones" (Psalm 30:4). "Sing to the LORD a new song, and His praise in the congregation of the godly ones" (Psalm 149:1).

> *Worship.* "Worship the LORD with reverence" (Psalm 2:11). "Worship the LORD in holy array" (Psalm 29:2).

> *Giving thanks.* "Give thanks to the LORD, for He is good" (Psalm 136:1).

> *Seeking Him.* "Seek the LORD and His strength; seek His face continually" (Psalm 105:4).

> *Bringing a gift.* "And they shall not appear before the LORD empty-handed. Every man shall give as he is able, according to the blessing of the LORD your God which He has given you" (Deuteronomy 16:16–17).

> *Waiting.* "Wait for the LORD; be strong, and let your heart take courage; yes, wait for the LORD" (Psalm 27:14).

› *Calling.* "Call to Me, and I will answer you, and I will tell you great and mighty things, which you do not know" (Jeremiah 33:3).

› *Casting your burdens upon Him.* "Cast your burden upon the LORD, and He will sustain you" (Psalm 55:22). "Casting all your anxiety upon Him, because He cares for you" (1 Peter 5:7).

› *Humbling yourself.* "Humble yourselves in the presence of the Lord, and He will exalt you" (James 4:10). "Humble yourselves, therefore, under the mighty hand of God, that He may exalt you at the proper time" (1 Peter 5:6).

› *Coming near.* "Draw near to God and He will draw near to you" (James 4:8).

These are just a few of the direct orders the Bible gives to show us how we should approach our God and what to give Him. The psalms especially are full of this type of instruction.

As we look at these verses, it becomes very obvious to us that God's need is for fellowship, closeness, love, our submission and a very direct involvement in our lives. He wants to care for, provide for, carry, bless and love us. The more we study our own needs and the needs God has, the more we come to the conclusion that we desperately need Him to meet our needs and He very much needs us to meet His.

Why is this? The Bible gives us the answer:

> For from Him and through Him and to Him are all things (Romans 11:36).

> For by him were all things created, that are in heaven, and that are in earth, visible and invisible, whether they be thrones, or dominions, or principalities, or powers: all things were created by him, and for him (Colossians 1:16, KJV).

In other words, we were not only made by Him, but for Him. That's why there is a perfect match between God and us and the ability to meet each other's needs. That is also why a man apart from God cannot fill his soul and find fulfillment in anything or anyone else as hard as he might try. There will always be an empty space that only God Himself can fill.

Are we qualified to meet God's needs? It makes us already feel uneasy to think that God has needs, but the thought that we ought to meet them is even more scary. If He is God, why does He need *me* to bless Him, love Him, praise Him, thank Him and make Him glad? Does heaven not have all of this and even more available? After all, the angels are able to present the most perfect worship, praise, adoration and music in the universe. Surely they can do it much better than I ever could (especially considering my musical ability!).

But again, our God is so different from our expectations. He actually wants our imperfect worship. Psalm 66:1 says, "Make a joyful noise unto God, all ye lands." He does not seem to be at all concerned with the sounds we make or the words we choose. Instead, He looks at our hearts. He enjoys knowing that we are so thankful and so full of love toward Him because He has redeemed us. We are capable of a depth of gratitude, love and worship that the angels don't have because they never were lost.

He is humble enough to accept and appreciate what I give Him. It is incredible to think that God not only wants and appreciates my imperfect worship and ministry to Him, but it actually does something for Him. Otherwise, the Bible would never tell us to do it. It meets His need for love and fellowship, it makes Him rejoice and be glad and it blesses Him.

Usually, the greater always blesses the lesser, but consider this: God Almighty has allowed Abraham, David and me to bless Him. It takes a lot of humility from our God to accept this from us and to enjoy it.

Because of this humility in the nature of God, I believe that Jesus would have accepted ministry to strengthen Him for His battles and for the cross, if someone would have offered it to Him.

Let me encourage you to get up in the morning or go to church with this attitude: "Today, I will bless my God, make Him glad, cause Him to rejoice, give Him my love and worship Him to meet His needs."

If we come to our God to meet His needs, we will never need to worry about leaving empty-handed. As we give to Him, He will look for ways to bless us abundantly.

JESUS CAME TO DO HIS FATHER'S WILL, NOT HIS OWN

How did Jesus manage to be so successful in His ministry? Every time He prayed, He got an answer. Every time He went to heal a person or to cast out a demon, it worked. He didn't have a success rate of 30 percent or 80 percent—not even 99 percent. He actually had a 100 percent success rate at all times.

I believe that there are many important factors involved in this, such as faith, obedience, believing the Word, knowing the right Scriptures, having a close relationship with God and knowing how to deal with people.

But there was one outstanding attitude that characterized and determined every part of Jesus' ministry:

I have come to do Thy will (Hebrews 10:9).

My food is to do the will of Him who sent Me (John 4:34).

Yet not My will, but Thine be done (Luke 22:42).

If Jesus would have chosen His own will, He might have been born in a palace instead of a stable. He might have associated with royalty, the ruling elders and the high priest instead of fishermen, tax collectors, former sinners and prostitutes. He might have traveled in a chariot or on horseback instead of walking around the dusty roads of Galilee, Judea and Samaria. He might have also looked for a more pleasant and less painful way to bear our sin and sickness than being tortured and hung on a cross.

The secret of Jesus' success was this: He first found out what His Father's will was, and then He simply did just that, leaving all His own wishes behind. And whatever the Father's will was, He did it joyfully and with all of His heart.

Jesus came to His mission field, totally abandoning His own will. To come with this attitude made Him accept discomfort, rejection, hunger, thirst, tiredness—and the cross—without complaint.

How often do we come to our mission field with expectations and plans that might not be God's thoughts at all? Then we complain and agonize, and try to manipulate God into blessing our desires and plans. Perhaps we want a good place to rent, a vehicle for our use, extra money to afford good food and an open door to preach freely.

But when we arrive, we instead find hostility from the people, no vehicle available for our team, no place to rent and very limited money. What will our reaction be?

Is it this? "Father, I came to do Thy will, and I accept whatever Your plans are for this moment. You sent me here; and if it is hardship You have chosen for right now, I am willing to trust Your wisdom."

Or do we pray in this way? "God, this is awful and not at all what I expected! If this situation doesn't change within 24 hours, I will leave this place and go somewhere else."

How much do you think our success rate in our ministry would improve if we, like Jesus, would enter the village with this attitude? "Father, I have come to do Thy will, whatever it may be." What would happen if we actually cared enough to find out exactly what His will was before rushing off to do something?

To Die, Not to Live

When Jesus was born into this world, it was for one purpose alone: to die as a sacrifice for our sin. Before the foundation of the world, God in His foreknowledge knew that mankind would fall and would need a redeemer—and Jesus agreed to be this redeemer: "[For you were redeemed] with precious blood, as of a lamb unblemished and spotless, the blood of Christ. For He was foreknown before the foundation of the world, but has appeared in these last times for the sake of you" (1 Peter 1:19-20).

As Jesus was growing up and then entered His ministry, He was fully aware of the purpose for His life: He had come to die, not to live!

> Just as the Son of Man did not come to be served, but to serve, and to give His life a ransom for many (Matthew 20:28).

> I am the good shepherd; the good shepherd lays down His life for the sheep (John 10:11).

When the people who witnessed His miracles wanted to make Jesus king, He simply walked away. You see, the cross was continually before His eyes, and the only goal He had for His life was to die!

When Jesus looked at the temporary attractions and comforts of life that could have been His, He chose to walk straight by them. They no longer had any value or pull on His heart because He had come to die—not to live.

The persecution, the hate, the rejection, the physical suffering as well as the mental agony that Jesus faced created no rebellion, resistance or self-pity in His heart. He had come with the goal to die, and what He faced was just part of this death. *Jesus had died to Himself and to His desires long before He ever died on the cross!* That's why all His decisions were able to line up with His purpose: to lay down His life.

He had made peace with His goal and purpose to die. Otherwise, He would have fought it with His power and with legions of angels. He was actually able to pray for those who crucified Him, "Father forgive them" (Luke 23:34).

When you followed God's call and you entered your ministry or your mission field, how did you come? With what purpose and goal did you arrive there? Was your goal to establish a great work for God, to become a significant leader, to use your gifts and talents for God, to save this village from hell, to make a name for yourself or to work toward making a decent living?

Or did you come to die?

Jesus said to His disciples, "As the Father has sent Me, I also send you" (John 20:21). The truth is, the Father sent Jesus to die, not to live.

It will be a very difficult decision for you to accept Christ's purpose and goal as your own. *You must make peace with your death before you are actually able to go and die!* If you don't, you will fight it—and fail.

If we neglect to make this decision, we will seek more than death. We will become anxious when we are not honored, when we are treated wrongly or when our needs are not met. When our expectations are not fulfilled, we will become discouraged, will lose our vision and our attitude of service and will want to go back. Our heart will become bitter and jealous of others, and we will end up being a hindrance.

Tremendous peace will take over in our lives if we have come to a place where we can say with all our heart: "I came to this village not to go back. I came to die—so they can live."

10

You Are Not
Your Own

A few years ago, when I was driving home from my work in our mission office, I felt very tired and I started to think:

"When I get home I will have no time to rest or even to sit down. There is so much work to do in the office and at home that I am not getting enough sleep. My husband has to travel so much, and I am alone here at home. And with all these responsibilities I have no time at all to do anything for myself."

As I thought about my situation, I felt sorry for myself, and I said to Jesus, "Lord, all these things are so hard." I expected Jesus to feel sorry for me as well, and I was hoping He would comfort me with a nice Bible verse. Maybe He would let me feel His wonderful presence there in the car.

But nothing like this happened at all. He responded to my words with something I didn't want to hear. This is what He told me: "You are not your own (1 Corinthians 6:19)! I have the right to ask you for *all* your strength, *all* your sleep, *all* your time, and for everything in your life."

I didn't like His answer, and I was disappointed that He

didn't seem to feel sorry for me. But His response reminded me once again of His ownership of me.

WE LIKE CHRIST'S OWNERSHIP—
IF IT IS FOR OUR BENEFIT

When we first get saved, we are so excited and happy that we now belong to Jesus and Jesus belongs to us. We discover that because we have a new Lord and Savior, we have received a wealth of wonderful blessings. Our sins are forgiven, every yoke that once bound us is broken, and the devil cannot touch or rule us any longer. We are full of joy, peace and happiness that is out of this world.

We have eternal life, our names are written in the Lamb's Book of Life, and we are on the way to heaven. Jesus loves us, He cares for our every need and He has promised never to leave us. He has given us the power of the Holy Spirit and the right to come boldly to His throne.

We find it truly wonderful to be a Christian, and we don't mind Christ's ownership at all. In fact, we like it—as long as it doesn't disturb our expectations of life or touch our own interests.

THE OTHER PART OF OWNERSHIP

This ownership deal reminds me of a rupee note. One glance will tell us how much it is worth: buying power = one rupee. However, when we look closer, we discover the legal part: "Government of India." This rupee is the property of India.

When we accepted Christ, we might have only desired to go to heaven or to find peace and joy. We never thought that we were the object of a legal transaction: We were transferred from the ownership of the devil to the ownership of Jesus Christ.

There is a legal side to this ownership. Because it concerns us, it is very important for us to know what and how much was paid, where the transaction took place and who did the buying. Furthermore, it is vital that we know which rights the owner has and if any rights are left for us!

To find the answers to all these questions, let us read the official bill of sale:

> Or do you not know that your body is a temple of the Holy Spirit who is in you, whom you have from God, and that you are not your own? For you have been bought with a price: therefore glorify God in your body (1 Corinthians 6:19–20).

> You were bought with a price; do not become slaves of men (1 Corinthians 7:23).

> You were not redeemed with perishable things like silver or gold from your futile way of life inherited from your forefathers, but with precious blood, as of a lamb unblemished and spotless, the blood of Christ (1 Peter 1:18–19).

> Do you not know that when you present yourselves to someone as slaves for obedience, you are slaves of the one whom you obey, either of sin resulting in death, or of obedience resulting in righteousness? . . . And having been freed from sin, you became slaves of righteousness (Romans 6:16, 18).

> But now having been freed from sin and enslaved to God . . . (Romans 6:22).

These verses tell us very clearly that as human beings, we are either under the rulership of the devil or we are owned by Jesus. There is no neutral position where we are free to ourselves. In either case, we have an owner and we are slaves.

As believers, we were bought with a price—the blood of Jesus. The bill was paid at the cross of Calvary, and Jesus Himself did the buying. These verses reveal very plainly that from the moment of purchase on, we were no longer our own—for always.

This means that Jesus holds the legal right to our lives, and we have become a possession of His.

To have a people for His own possession was always God's desire and plan from the beginning of creation:

You shall be My own possession (Exodus 19:5).

. . . to be a people for His own possession (Deuteronomy 4:20).

This desire of God was fulfilled when Jesus bought us. We have become this people of His own possession. First Peter 2:9 confirms this clearly: "But you are a chosen race, a royal priesthood, a holy nation, a people for God's own possession, that you may proclaim the excellencies of Him who has called you out of darkness into His marvelous light."

After evaluating all these verses we have read, it definitely looks as though Jesus owns every part of us, and we have nothing left for ourselves. He received every single right, and we have none!

What does it mean to be owned? It is very difficult for us to imagine that we have an owner because we no longer have slavery in our society. Nowadays we may perhaps have hired servants in our fields. But that is not the same.

Servants have rights, they are not owned and they work for wages. They are protected by laws and can demand reasonable working conditions. After they finish their job, they can collect their pay and go home and live their lives as they please.

Slaves were different. Their masters bought them from a trader for an agreed price at the marketplace. As soon as the transaction was completed, the slave became the property of his master. He had no rights at all. He couldn't ask for anything—even food, a bed to sleep in or an extra piece of clothing. He had to accept whatever his master saw fit to give him. If the master sent his slave to work for 12 hours in the field or told him to sleep on the dirt floor, the slave had no right to say "no" or even to question his owner's decision. The master could even kill him if he wanted to, because the life and death of his slave were in his hands. The slave could not expect any gratitude, salary or vacation for his services.

The slave might have had many wishes, dreams and desires for his own life, but he had to give them all up, including his own will, because he had a master who owned him.

Whether we like it or not, we have been bought just like this slave. This was the only way we could be redeemed from hell.

Thinking of ourselves as a piece of property or a possession is not very appealing, but that is exactly what we are according to the Word of God. We totally belong to Jesus, and as owner He does not need to share us with anyone: not with the world, the devil or even with our own selves!

At any time, Jesus can walk up to us and say,

> You are My possession, because I bought you with My blood. It is My right to ask you now for all your strength, your health, all your time, your sleep, your comfortable life, your house and all your money and possessions, to be used to advance My cause. I also ask for your husband or wife and your children, to serve Me full-time on a pioneer field. Finally, it is My right to ask you not only to give everything you have, but also to lay down your own life for the Gospel, and die as a martyr somewhere in Bhutan or Nepal.
>
> You have no choices left in your life, and I don't need to ask your permission, because nothing you have is your own anymore. I can use it all as I please. You will never again belong to yourself or do your own thing.

How does this sound? Is it frightening? Legally, Jesus has the absolute right to demand whatever He wants from us! But our God is truly amazing. He doesn't claim His right by force.

God doesn't demand His right of ownership. Throughout the Bible, we see that God has the right of ownership on our lives. He could demand and force us to submit to Him, but He doesn't do that.

You see, our God is a loving God who gives us the choice to determine what we want to do. In His heart, He longs and waits for us to choose Him, but He is willing to abide by our decision. This doesn't sound very profitable for Him, and He runs the risk that most of us would rather decide to have our own freedom.

The devil is never as generous. Whatever he gets in his hands, he keeps by force.

Do you remember when Jesus called His disciples? He walked along the seashore and saw Peter and Andrew, and later James and John, mending their nets. As He passed by their boats, all He called out to them was, "Follow Me." Then he walked off.

As the Son of God, Jesus had all power to back up His words. He could have turned to Peter and the others and said, "You follow Me, or I will cause lightning to strike you dead." Peter and his friends would have been so scared that they would have gladly left their boats to go with Jesus. But Jesus didn't do anything like that. He only gave them an invitation to submit to His rightful ownership.

We see the same thing in the Old Testament at the time when Joshua was old and knew he would die soon. He assembled the leaders of Israel and told them, "Choose for yourselves today whom you will serve" (Joshua 24:15).

The most amazing part of this story is that after all God had done for Israel in Egypt, in the wilderness and in the conquest of Canaan, He still asked them to choose. They owed Him everything they were and everything they had. He delivered them from slavery, saved them from their enemies, did miracles for them, fed them with manna for 40 years and gave them the

Promised Land. Without God they wouldn't have even been alive. Yet this story shows us the heart of our God. He had all the right in the world to own these people, yet He still asked them to choose to whom they would submit and serve.

Love does not take advantage of ownership. In India, as well as in the surrounding countries, there are many temples and shrines of various deities. Some of the images of these gods look quite dangerous, angry and threatening. One of them has a bow and arrow, another one is surrounded by snakes and a third has all the decapitated heads of his enemies hung around his neck. One of the Nepali deities is pictured slaying his enemy by tearing out his bowels.

Can you imagine being owned by a god like this? How frightening and risky it must be to submit yourself to such a deity. One day he might be pleased with you and bless you, and the next day he might not like what you do and will curse you, destroy your crops or kill you.

What a contrast to Jesus our God, who gave His life, willingly hanging on the cross to redeem us! Jesus is love, and love never takes advantage of ownership. First Corinthians 13:4-7 gives us a clear understanding of the nature of our God:

> Love is patient, love is kind, and is not jealous; love does not brag and is not arrogant, does not act unbecomingly; it does not seek its own, is not provoked, does not take into account a wrong suffered, does not rejoice in unrighteousness, but rejoices with the truth; bears all things, believes all things, hopes all things, endures all things.

We have no reason to fear His ownership! Jesus would never harm us for His own amusement. He is not planning to take away our happiness and rob us of the things we love. He doesn't enjoy making us miserable or punishing us, and He does not seek to destroy us.

It is absolutely safe to submit to Him. We will experience His love in an even greater way as we decide to totally abandon ourselves into His hands. God is looking for people who willingly recognize His ownership and accept it as their choice of life.

Understanding total ownership creates a willingness to be spent. I believe that if we truly understand the meaning of salvation, then we will also understand the privilege of placing all our rights into the hands of the One who purchased us with His own blood.

The apostle Paul was such a man. He understood very well what salvation and ownership meant, and he made the choice out of his own free will to become a bondservant of Christ, which literally means a slave for life.

Paul shared in some of his letters about his understanding of Christ's ownership of his life. At the moment of his salvation, he accepted this ownership fully and freely. He explained how this relationship affected his personal life and ministry and especially his attitude toward others. In his writings he has given us some very clear and practical examples of how much and how freely God was able to use him as a result of this total submission: "And I will most *gladly spend* and be expended for your souls" (2 Corinthians 12:15). Paul said here, "I belong to the Lord. He is my owner. I am so very glad—and it is my greatest joy if He takes my life and spends it for the souls of others."

Do you realize that Paul did *not* say, "I am glad if God *uses* my life." *Spending* involves much more than *using*. It looks as though the more God spent him, the more Paul was glad: "But even if *I am being poured out* as a drink offering upon the sacrifice and *service of your faith,* I rejoice and share my joy with you all" (Philippians 2:17).

Paul saw himself as a pitcher with water in it. God took this pitcher in His hand and began pouring the water out over the lives of others so they could see Jesus. Paul stood by and watched God pour out his life. He rejoiced greatly because his goal was that God would spend him, pour him out and sacrifice him—so that others might live.

Paul didn't complain, "God, you are pouring out too much of me. Half of me is already gone! It gets too hard. I wish I had earned that degree instead. I would be sitting now in Jerusalem with the elders, ruling the nation, and I would have a better life." Instead, this is what he told the believers in Thessalonica: "We were *well-pleased to impart* to you not only the gospel of God but also *our own lives*" (1 Thessalonians 2:8).

Paul not only wanted to preach to these people, but he wanted to invest his life in them as well. Practically, this meant a lot of trouble and effort. It took time, hard work, counseling, teaching, bearing burdens, prayers, tears and great commitment: For this reason *I endure all things* for the sake of those who are chosen" (2 Timothy 2:10).

God didn't need to be careful about what He asked from Paul. Paul had already told his Master, "Lord, You can ask from me whatever it takes to serve others, build them up and get them to heaven. I will not complain, and I will hold nothing back. You can spend and pour out my life until there is not even one drop left. I will rejoice greatly if You pour out my life totally for Your purpose."

Paul not only said or wrote all these things—he lived them. If you want to see what it actually looked like when God poured out Paul's life, you need to read 2 Corinthians 11:23–28:

> Are they servants of Christ? (I speak as if insane) I more so; in far more labors, in far more imprisonments, beaten times without number, often in danger of death. Five times I received from the Jews thirty-nine lashes. Three times I was beaten with rods, once I was stoned, three times I was ship-

wrecked, a night and a day I have spent in the deep. I have
been on frequent journeys, in dangers from rivers, dangers
from robbers, dangers from my countrymen, dangers from
the Gentiles, dangers in the city, dangers in the wilderness,
dangers on the sea, dangers among false brethren; I have
been in labor and hardship, through many sleepless nights,
in hunger and thirst, often without food, in cold and expo-
sure. Apart from such external things, there is the daily pressure upon me of concern for all the churches.

Throughout the Bible, we see that God always looked for a
man or a woman whose life He could pour out in order for His
people to be saved.

In the Old Testament, God found Moses. He completely
spent Moses' life for the deliverance and survival of Israel.
When God poured out Moses' life on behalf of Israel, there was
nothing left. It cost him his position in Egypt, his throne, his
education, his strength and his life.

In Exodus 17:11, we see Moses as an older man. But he still
had the same attitude and willingness to be spent and poured
out for Israel. Israel was in a fierce battle with Amalek. Moses
knew they needed his intercession. He climbed a mountain and
held up his hands, praying many hours for their victory. His arms
became tired, and he was exhausted. Hur and Aaron helped him,
holding up his hands until the victory was won. What a picture
of a servant of God who is willing to be poured out completely.

In Exodus 32, we read that the people of Israel had sinned
so greatly that God was about to finish them off, blot them out
of His book and kill them all. In verse 32 we see Moses pleading
with God: "But now, if Thou wilt, forgive their sin—and if not,
please blot me out from Thy book which Thou hast written!"

Moses was willing to intercede. He put his life on the line
and spent himself for the people of Israel. God heard him and
extended His mercy.

God didn't stop with Moses. In each generation that followed, He called out those who would allow Him to pour out their lives in order to call His people to Him—the living God. Among them were leaders like Joshua and David, prophets like Samuel, Jeremiah, Isaiah and Daniel, as well as many others whose names are not known to us.

God the Father not only spent people for His purpose. He also gave His only Son Jesus to be completely poured out and spent for a lost and dying world. Everything Jesus had and owned He laid down. He willingly died and gave His blood as the price for our redemption.

After His resurrection, when Jesus established His Church, He followed the same pattern: He looked for men and women who understood and accepted His ownership of their lives and who had no reservations of being poured out and spent for the Body of Christ.

Think about the apostles. All of them except one died as martyrs. Many of the early Christians paid the same price.

The history of missions tells us the same story. God found men and women whose lives He was allowed to pour out for nations that had never before heard His name. Many of these men and women suffered greatly and died on the field for the sake of the Gospel.

God poured out Hudson Taylor for China, Adoniram Judson for Myanmar, William Carey and Amy Carmichael for India, Jim Elliot for the Auca Indians in Ecuador and Sadhu Sundar Singh for India and Tibet.

Today as you look at the map of your own country of India, Nepal, Myanmar, Sri Lanka, Bhutan or China, you will find thousands of villages without a church or a single Gospel witness. Every day multitudes of people die and go to hell without ever hearing the name of Jesus Christ even one time.

God is looking for men and women He can send to those

villages, those who have understood and accepted His owner-ship and are ready to be poured out.

Jesus doesn't want to preserve us; He wants to spend us. One day after my husband had spoken in a church service, a young man approached him and told him that he would like to join our ministry. He was eager to learn what he would have to do if he worked in our mission office.

My husband started with the most important part. He told him of our daily prayer times before work, our Tuesday night prayer fellowship, our monthly all-night prayer meeting and other special prayer times as needs arose.

This young man became very frightened. He looked at my husband and asked, "You mean, if I join you, I have to pray like this?" My husband told him, "Brother, you stay in your local church and learn some more, and maybe think about joining us later."

This young man was willing to do something for God, as well as enjoy the benefits of working in a Christian ministry, but he was not willing to pour out his life. The same thing can be said about thousands of believers who know the Lord and even about many who have studied in a Bible school and want to serve Him full-time. They want Jesus to give them a good life and the honor of being a pastor. They would like to wear a nice *yuba*, carry a big Bible and an umbrella and go to nice houses to pray.

But God is not looking for people to fill a position or to be honored and revered. He does not even look for those who can preach well or those who are able to accomplish great things. He has enough of those already. He is looking for people like Paul, whose lives He can pour out until no drop is left.

Sometimes when I visit certain homes, I can see nice teacups sitting on a special shelf in the living room. Some of them are beautifully decorated and look very costly. But when teatime comes, to my surprise, my tea doesn't arrive in one of those expensive cups. It comes in an ordinary glass.

Why? You see, the teacups on that shelf are for display only— not for use. God has no interest in taking our lives and putting them in a showcase like those teacups so that everyone can look at us and admire the degree we received from Bible school.

The world is going to hell—time is running out for millions of people. God doesn't want to waste time to show us off. He longs to spend us for the salvation of millions.

You are not able to give yourself to be spent if you love the world. Even if we are willing to go as pioneer missionaries to North India, Nepal or Tibet, God cannot use us fully and effectively unless we are willing to be totally spent. And that can only happen when we, like Paul, become bondservants for life, fully accepting Christ's ownership.

You see, anything less than this restricts God in His movement, His plan and His power. Every time He would want to do something, He would have to ask our permission first if He might use us. We are a risk to God's kingdom because our unsubmitted position requires Him to consult us and make detours in His plans to accommodate our unwillingness. We might actually be the greatest hindrance for a mighty outpouring of God's Spirit over our nation.

Why is it that only a handful of believers ever make a commitment like Paul, totally submitting themselves to Christ's ownership? And why is it that out of those who make it, only very few stay with it for life?

Is it fear? Is it that His requests are too hard and too demanding? Is their family opposed to it? Perhaps all of these are reasons we could consider. But I believe the biggest reason is found in 1 John 2:15: "Do not love the world, nor the things in the world. If any one loves the world, the love of the Father is not in him."

The love of the Father is a totally giving love. John 3:16 says, "For God so loved the world, that He gave His only begotten Son, that whoever believes in Him should not perish, but have eternal life."

This giving love of the Father not only gave us Jesus, but poured Him out to redeem us from our sins. This love caused God to hold nothing back but to give all He had. The reason why we do not submit to God's ownership and why we are not willing to be spent is because this giving love of the Father is not in us. We love the world instead.

Many of us are very inconsistent in our commitment and our willingness to submit to Christ's ownership. One day we allow Him to pour us out, and the next day we fight it.

If there is a battle in your heart over whether you want to be spent or not, it simply reveals that you still have too much love of the world in you and too little love of the Father! Paul didn't talk about any such battle in his heart at all. He only spoke about the great joy he had to be poured out. The reason he could say this was because the love of the Father in him was greater than the love of the world.

God desires to spend all of us. When God calls us to serve Him and to submit to His ownership, He doesn't have a part-time ownership contract in mind that will run out after 2, 10 or 30 years. His plan is Revelation 2:10: "Be faithful until death, and I will give you the crown of life."

The Lord desires, just as He did for Paul's life, not to spend a little of us, but to spend all of us and pour us out completely—for the rest of our lives on earth.

Sometimes we come to a point in our lives at which we say to ourselves and to God, "It is enough now. I have been poured out as much as I can handle. I am too tired to go on like this. I have sacrificed, suffered and worked much more than others. Twenty or 40 years of service are plenty. Now let me have a few years of my own life; let me enjoy my family and have some rest. Let others do the work now."

God, however, thinks differently. He searches for people who, like Paul, consider it a joy if God pours out their lives continuously until their death.

What we are really doing and saying is more than desiring some rest. We are looking back after putting our hands to the plow (Luke 9:62). The devil tries to stop us from being continuously willing, because he knows what the result would be. We must pray much for one another, that we will stay willing to be spent.

If Jesus would have thought like us, He would have said something like this: "Father, 33 years on this earth is enough hardship. I have poured out My life for almost three years of ministry. It is sufficient, and I am coming home now."

Do you know what would have happened if Jesus would have thought like we do? He never would have died! He would have said, "It is enough" after they scourged Him, mocked Him and pushed the crown of thorns down on His head. Or at the very latest, after they nailed Him to the cross, He would have stopped the whole thing and ascended to heaven.

But Jesus didn't do that. Even while He was hanging on the cross for many hours, He never looked back but remained willing to be spent. He said to His Father, "Father, You are allowed to pour out My life until every drop of My blood is gone." Jesus stayed willing until His life was finished and our salvation completed.

Our salvation didn't depend on Jesus' teaching, His power to heal, His anointing for ministry, His miracles or His authority over demons. It depended on His willingness to die.

Millions of people—whole nations—are bound in darkness. If they are to hear the Gospel and be able to call upon Jesus for salvation, it will not depend on our critical studies in theology, our ability to debate, our strategies and plans or our degrees. *It will depend on nothing less than our willingness to be poured out until death.*

In John 12:24 Jesus says, "Unless a grain of wheat falls into the earth and dies, it remains by itself alone; but if it dies, it bears much fruit." If we desire to become this grain of wheat that brings much fruit, we must accept Christ's ownership of our lives and be willing to be poured out until our death has taken place.

11

WHAT MY GOD SAYS, THAT I WILL SPEAK

*I*t is the most exciting and amazing reality to comprehend that the Almighty God, who created the vastness of the universe, has called us to serve Him and to proclaim His eternal Word. If we even remotely understand the significance of our calling, we will come to the conclusion that no president or king in this world has a higher office than the one we have received. There are some very important facts to remember that will greatly help us stay on course as we fulfill our service.

YOU ARE ONLY A MESSENGER

God never searches for an adviser, editor or scriptwriter to help Him with composing His will for mankind. He always looks for a simple *mouthpiece or channel* He can use to convey His Word. Every time God calls someone to deliver a message to His own people or to the world, He makes this fact very clear. Here are some examples of what God expects of His messengers:

Moses: "Now then go, and I, even I, will be with your mouth, and teach you what you are to say" (Exodus 4:12).

Jeremiah: "Do not say, 'I am a youth,' because everywhere I send you, you shall go, and all that I command you, you shall speak. . . . Behold, I have put My words in your mouth. . . . Now, gird up your loins, and arise, and speak to them all which I command you" (Jeremiah 1:7, 9, 17).

Ezekiel: "But you shall speak My words to them whether they listen or not. . . . Son of man, I have appointed you a watchman to the house of Israel; whenever you hear a word from My mouth, warn them from Me" (Ezekiel 2:7, 3:17).

The apostles: ". . . teaching them to observe all that I commanded you" (Matthew 28:20).

THE MESSAGE IS NOT YOURS

Whether you preach, teach, exhort, counsel or prophesy, you must remember the message is not your own. This means that because it does not originate with you, you have no right to change its content in order to fit denominational traditions, cultural issues or personal preferences.

You also have no right *not* to deliver the message—if God has truly sent you. This would be outright disobedience, such as in Jonah's case when he was supposed to go to Nineveh and he sailed off to Tarsus instead.

If you are not sure that what is in your heart is actually God's message for a situation or for someone, please wait. Pray, and first make certain before you speak a word.

Never abuse your office as a messenger. This is especially important when people have come to expect a "special word from the Lord" through you, because you have acquired a reputation of having an anointed ministry or a gift.

Don't ever allow yourself to proclaim something in the name of the Lord that has come out of the imagination of your own heart. Fear of disappointing your audience or losing their respect and honor are never good enough reasons to compromise your obedience and fabricate something that God never said.

Abraham and some of the prophets often had years go by between revelations, yet they would not have dared to make one up just to impress their friends or scare their enemies. In Old Testament times, if a person falsified a message, made one up in the name of Jehovah, or if the prophecy didn't come to pass, the penalty was death by execution.

I believe that God has His own reasons for not giving a special word every time people want one. Often you will find that believers don't want to search the Scripture, spend time in prayer and seek the Lord's face for themselves. They find it much more convenient and less troublesome to get their answers from a servant of God who does the "work" for them. However, God's desire is that His people learn to hear His voice and apply Scripture to their own lives.

Don't let yourself be pressured into meddling with God's message!

YOU ARE STILL DUST

Even the most amazing revelations, prophecies and messages that you deliver on behalf of God Almighty will not elevate you to the position of a super being. We have this treasure—Jesus—in an earthen vessel (see 2 Corinthians 4:7). We will always remain an earthen vessel, and we are still dust in spite of the glory and the message placed inside us.

If God uses us to speak on His behalf, to preach His Word or to perform a miracle, it will definitely affect our walk with Him, our faith, our commitment, our burden, our love for Him and so on; but it will not change our dust into gold. If we can only remember that after the message we remain the same earthen vessel as we were before, it will keep us from destructive pride, self-glorification and people worship.

God does ask us to hold in honor those who teach the Word, and we must do so. But throughout history, Christianity made terrible mistakes by elevating mere messengers to almost god-like positions. Knowing that you are just an earthen vessel will greatly help you stay humble, and it will give you the freedom to become a servant to all—just as Jesus was. You won't have to worry about wearing distinctive clothes to advertise your high position or holiness. You can even do regular manual work without losing your glory. It won't matter any longer whether you are given a place of honor at a banquet or if you eat from a tea shop on the street corner.

A few years ago while traveling in Kerala, I saw something that still remains very vivid in my mind. In front of us at a street intersection was a jeep that obviously had engine trouble and wouldn't start. One man was pushing the vehicle, while the driver made every effort to start it up.

However, the unusual thing was that while this man pushed, exhausted and sweating, a third man was sitting in the vehicle—doing absolutely nothing. He wore distinctive robes and a headdress, marking him as some kind of bishop or high-ranking church official within a respected Christian denomination.

Why didn't he help push the vehicle? I think that his high position, dignity and the robes he wore prevented him from engaging in such dirty work.

Later on I thought that if Jesus had been sitting in that jeep, He surely would have jumped out, pulled up His tunic and helped with the pushing. He was a servant of all and, as such, was not afraid to get dirty or behave like an ordinary man.

YOU CANNOT DIVORCE THE MESSAGE
FROM YOUR LIFE

The message you proclaim only becomes valid and believable to your audience when you live it, act on it and portray it before the world in your everyday life. People must see the Gospel at the same time that they hear it.

For example, let us say that you preached on Ephesians 5:25

in your Sunday service: "Husbands, love your wives, just as Christ also loved the church and gave Himself up for her."

After your sermon, you came home and found that your wife was not feeling well. You sat down and demanded your dinner to be served right now. You clearly expressed your dissatisfaction with her because she only cooked two dishes instead of three.

After eating your food, you went to your room to spend the next two hours reading your Bible, praying and singing worship songs. Then you visited your neighbor's house to talk and drink tea.

During these hours, your wife had to wash the dishes, feed and bathe three small children, put them to bed, prepare lunch for school tomorrow and finally wash clothes for everyone. When you returned from your neighbor's house, you asked her, "Why didn't you rest if you are not well?"

What do you think your church members and neighbors learned that day from your sermon as they watched how it was practically applied in their pastor's life? How much do you think God was impressed by your two hours of Bible reading and prayer as you completely failed to show understanding, love and compassion to your wife?

You are supposed to treat her as Jesus treats the Church, willing to lay down His life for her. You didn't say a kind word to her all afternoon, and you didn't even ask her if you could help her with something so she could rest. Maybe you think you are willing to die for her, but you are not even willing to risk embarrassment before your neighbors if they should see you helping your wife with the home and the children.

Have you ever noticed how Jesus touched the lepers, talked to the woman at the well, comforted the widows, took time for the children and ate dinner with the socially outcast? He actually violated the cultural and religious barriers of His time in order to communicate how God loves. He was more concerned about showing His message practically than about what people would think of Him. As the Son of God, He even lowered Himself to the position of a slave and didn't feel embarrassed to wash the feet of His disciples.

There is great liberty when we remember that we are just earthen vessels and that if Jesus could be a servant without losing face, then we can too!

Perhaps you preached on James 2:1–9. The content of your message was this: Before God, all men are equal, and we too must treat them that way.

The next Sunday morning, the bank director of the town came to your church for the first time. As he entered the door, a beggar from the street with dirty clothes slipped in as well. What was your reaction to both?

You personally went to greet the bank director and offered him a nice padded chair in the front row, just beside the elders of the church. At the same time, you motioned the beggar to sit on the floor beside the door. You made sure that the fan blew cool air where the bank director sat, but the thought never crossed your mind that the beggar might be hot too. After the service, you sent your son to bring tea and sweets, and you invited the bank director to your parsonage; but the beggar left without being offered even a glass of water.

Let me ask you: What did you practically teach your church? You taught them with your mouth that they need to treat everyone equally, just as God does. But with your actions you instructed them to uphold the same barriers between castes and races, rich and poor, that your society has erected.

Always remember this: You are not only a speaking messenger, but a living instruction as well. You cannot divorce the message from your life without canceling out its effect on the people to whom you proclaim it.

You Are Not Above Counsel

This is an area in which many have gone wrong. As messengers of God, we are obligated to operate within biblical limits and the regulations He has given in His Word.

Paul clearly outlines that none of us is self-sufficient or above everyone else. We are all parts of one body, needing each other for survival, completion and correction. The Body of Christ has been given offices and gifts by the Lord that all work together to build up the Church. Each believer has a vital part in this body and is called on to exercise his or her responsibility.

The church, especially the leaders, elders and mature believers, are obligated to measure each proclamation, interpretation, teaching or prophecy with the already revealed, unchanging Word of God and to judge its accuracy accordingly. This must be done for the protection of the church and the protection of the messenger.

If the church fails to do this, two things will happen:

1. *False doctrines will go unchecked and can easily infiltrate the church and destroy it.*

2. *The messenger has no one who cares enough to help him stay on the right course.*

Paul subjected himself and his teaching to the judgment of the apostles and the church in Jerusalem. He had received more revelation on many subjects than they, but he found it right and absolutely necessary to subject himself and his message to their discernment:

> Then after an interval of fourteen years I went up again to Jerusalem with Barnabas, taking Titus along also. And it was because of a revelation that I went up; and I submitted to them the gospel which I preach among the Gentiles, but I did so in private to those who were of reputation, for fear that I might be running, or had run, in vain (Galatians 2:1–2).

A messenger might have the best of intentions to preach and teach the Word of God accurately. However, sometimes the message might be mixed with personal opinions or traditions, and it is the duty of the church to help the messenger align his message with the rest of the Word of God and to clarify its meaning.

There is great wisdom in the counsel of men and women of God who have walked with the Lord and who have proved themselves faithful with their lives and ministries. If you are questioned, corrected and helped by these kinds of people, please don't ever look on it as persecution or resist it. It is the love of God in action on your behalf! None of us, even if we live to be 100 years old, knows and understands all there is to know and understand about Scripture.

If men like David, Peter and Paul needed someone to check their lives, we surely need it too!

The danger occurs not so much when we first start out to serve the Lord. At that time we have our pastor, Bible school teacher or our team leader, who knows us well and cares enough to speak the truth in love to us. The real danger comes when we have our own ministry and we answer to no one, because all others are under our leadership.

At that point, we *must* remember that we are dust. It is true, God's glory is in us, but the devil will not rest until the moment after we are dead to try to trip us up and make us useless.

This is what you must do to protect yourself, your message and the work that has been entrusted to you: Make yourself deliberately accountable to other godly leaders, elders, pastors or mature believers. Give them the freedom to speak the truth in love. Set your relationship up with them in such a way that your life can be checked and you stay motivated to walk in the light with your personal life, your finances and your message. Allow them to counsel you before you make decisions, to pray with you and to correct you if necessary.

My husband has faithful leaders like these to call upon for advice and prayer. They are a great blessing and help to him, because he knows their counsel is based on a true concern for God's kingdom.

Many times I watch my husband dial the phone to ask for advice or prayer from these men before making decisions. Among these are some faithful brothers who will come and spend a day in prayer with him when burdens become too heavy and decisions so difficult. I am very thankful that he has such a group of godly men, because I have seen the great strength they have been for him and for the ministry.

It takes humility on your part to subject yourself to others, but in the long run, this is your best protection.

DON'T SET OUT TO DESTROY
THE BODY OF CHRIST

It is one thing to preach to unbelievers and challenge them to repent and accept Jesus Christ even at the cost of losing the whole world. But it is another thing to preach to born-again believers who love the Lord and have their basic doctrines correct but who have different views on church issues and scriptural interpretations.

We are called to walk in the light we have received from the Lord. However, each of us comes from a different background, denomination, tradition, culture and experience. All of us are on a spiritual journey, learning to walk with Jesus. Some have just started out. Others have known the Lord for 30 years.

This means that each of us is on a different level of spiritual development and understanding. It takes great wisdom, care and patience from a pastor to lead all these believers to spiritual maturity and to bring them to the point at which each takes on the image of Christ.

As a Bible school graduate or young evangelist, you might

have quite an understanding of certain issues in the Bible. You are eager to see your church accept your message, leaving traditions and denominational barriers behind.

This may actually happen, and the Lord might use you in a mighty way to bring revival to your church. However, if they don't accept your message and if none of them sees things your way, what are your plans then?

Whatever you decide, please do not set out to destroy the Body of Christ! As servants of God, our task is to fight the devil and destroy his kingdom, *not* to fight our brothers and tear down the Church for whom Jesus died. Before you condemn these believers or write them off, consider this:

> They are bought by the blood of Jesus.

> They are your brothers and sisters.

> They are precious in the sight of God.

> You will spend eternity together with them.

> You are commanded to love them and, if necessary, to lay down your life for them.

> You are asked to bear their burdens and their weaknesses.

> You are called to build them up.

> You are asked to regard them as higher than yourself.

I am not asking you as a messenger of God to compromise your convictions or your message. I am only asking you to love and accept your brother and your sister in the same way that God loves and accepts you.

You do not know every spiritual mystery there is, and you haven't achieved perfection, yet God is not afraid to accept you fully—in Jesus. You as well must fully accept your brother in Jesus, even if he has no insight in some of the areas that you do.

Who knows, he may be way ahead of you in other aspects. Give him time to grow. God is the One who started the work in him, and He is able to perfect it.

Please remember: You do not win someone over to your side by force and division. Jesus won us over to follow Him by laying down His life for us.

What should you practically do, then, if your message is not accepted?

1. *Make sure that the message you present is theologically accurate.* Many people will be scared off if your presentation has theological gaps and errors, even if your issue is the truth. Take counsel if necessary and know the Word of God.

2. *Don't try to preach or teach your message to these believers by force and cause divisions.* Instead, with all humility and love, live your message before their eyes. This is more convincing and convicting, and it speaks louder than any words ever could.

3. *Pray diligently that God will show them the truth.*

4. *Don't withdraw your fellowship and love* from believers who think differently about traditions of dress, dowry, jewelry, forms of worship, in-filling of the Holy Spirit, missions, interpretation of certain Scriptures, end-time events and so on. If they are born again, you are commanded to love them regardless, so the world will recognize you and them as followers of Christ (John 13:35).

5. *If they feel uncomfortable and threatened around you, they might ask you to leave their fellowship. If that happens, leave in love not in bitterness.* Keep your conscience clear and give no room to thoughts of retaliation. As for you, have peace with all of them (Romans 12:18). If they once again seek your fellowship later on, accept them with joy.

6. *If there is anything to judge, let God do the judging.* Remember, you are only appointed as a messenger, not as chairman of the High Court.

In our GFA headquarters in India, we have set aside every first Friday of the month as an all-night prayer meeting for missions. Up to 2,000 pastors and believers (men and women) from different groups and churches gather together for prayer.

Many of these believers never thought they could cross denominational borders and worship with members of other groups. But as they come, they discover the joy of being one in Jesus. Many have learned to love one another, lift up each other's burdens and come together joyfully before the throne of Jesus, who gave His life for all of them. There is great power in such unity, and we have seen the hand of God move in a mighty way on many mission fields as a result.

THERE IS A TIME TO STAND ALONE

For a messenger sent by God, there might very well come a time in his life when he has to stand alone for the truth, even at the risk of his life. Throughout the Bible we find such servants of God who had the boldness and uncompromising commitment to the One who sent them to be faithful, regardless of the outcome.

Noah was the only one of his entire generation who was righteous. He preached with his life for 120 years without winning one person over to Jehovah, the true and only God.

When **Joshua and Caleb** returned from spying out Canaan, they stood against the whole nation of Israel, which refused to go any further but wanted to go back to Egypt.

Daniel didn't pray to Darius, but to Jehovah alone. He accepted the risk of being thrown into the lions' den.

Shadrach, Meshach and Abed-nego were the only ones who didn't bow down to Nebuchadnezzar's image. They chose to be thrown into the fiery furnace rather than compromise.

David dared to fight Goliath because he believed that God would be with him, despite the fact that the whole army of Israel and their king were afraid and convinced it couldn't be done.

Elijah, on Mount Carmel, challenged 400 priests of Baal and all the people of Israel to test who was the true God—the One who answers by fire.

Jeremiah preached and prophesied to people who didn't repent and who didn't want to hear his message.

John the Baptist confronted King Herod of his sin and was beheaded as a result.

Stephen, the deacon, spoke the truth to the council and elders in Jerusalem—and was stoned for his refusal to compromise.

The apostles and early Christians witnessed for Jesus at the risk of losing their lives. Many of them were martyred, thrown to the wild animals in the Circus at Rome, burned alive and hung on crosses.

Martin Luther dared to proclaim "salvation by faith alone" in the face of a Christianity that had altogether lost this truth.

Out of all these heroes of faith who stood alone against the tide, I am often personally challenged by the life and words of the prophet **Micaiah**, found in chapter 18 of 2 Chronicles. Throughout his ministry, Micaiah probably lived with an axe held over his head and one foot in the grave. He was called by God to speak the truth to the most ungodly king Israel ever had: Ahab. The Bible gives Ahab this testimony:

> And Ahab the son of Omri did evil in the sight of the LORD more than all who were before him. And it came about, as though it had been a trivial thing for him to walk in the sins of Jeroboam the son of Nebat, that he married Jezebel the daughter of Ethbaal king of the Sidonians, and went to serve Baal and worshiped him. So he erected an altar for Baal in the house of Baal, which he built in Samaria. And Ahab also made the Asherah. Thus Ahab did more to provoke the LORD God of Israel than all the kings of Israel who were before him (1 Kings 16:30–33).

Jezebel, Ahab's wife, was absolutely wicked. Whomever she disliked was executed. Even Elijah once ran from her wrath.

The majority of the people of Israel had left the God of Israel and had indulged themselves in idol worship, especially of Asherah and of Baal, which Jezebel had brought into Israel. The worship of these gods caused Israel to embrace every sin of immorality and pagan practices. There were very few left who remained faithful to Jehovah, and most of those stayed in hiding to save themselves.

It was the worst time to be a prophet, and it was extremely dangerous to be sent to Ahab and Jezebel to confront them with their sins. The king, as well as the people, didn't want to hear the truth. In fact, when Micaiah was called on by Ahab, he was outnumbered 400 to 1. Ahab's 400 prophets always proclaimed the opposite of Micaiah's message. On top of this, Ahab hated Micaiah because of the unfavorable messages he fearlessly delivered (2 Chronicles 18:7).

Micaiah knew well that every time he was ordered to appear before Ahab, it might cost him his head. However, we find him to be a messenger who did not regard his life as dear unto himself but who was determined to be a mouthpiece through whom God could speak anything He chose.

In 2 Chronicles 18:12, the officer who picked up Micaiah for his audience with Ahab begged him to align his message with that of the other 400 prophets. Perhaps he wanted to save Micaiah's life, or he possibly feared a serious confrontation between King Ahab and King Jehoshaphat, who was visiting from Judah.

However, without hesitation, Micaiah answered him with a statement that revealed the commitment of his life: "As the LORD lives, what my God says, that I will speak" (2 Chronicles 18:13).

When Micaiah stood before Ahab and Jehoshaphat, he actually mocked Ahab by telling him to go to war and succeed. However, the ungodly king knew this prophet too well from previous encounters, and he asked for the truth in the name of the Lord.

In the following verses, Micaiah prophesied not only the defeat of Ahab's army but also the king's death. He went even further and explained in detail to spiritually blind Ahab the events that had taken place in the spirit world. He pointed out the deadly deception Ahab was caught in. With this explanation, the prophet actually gave Ahab a last chance to repent and escape death. We recognize clearly how much Micaiah desired to call this wicked king and the people of Israel back to the living God.

The fierce encounter that followed between Zedekiah, one of the false prophets, and Micaiah shows how certain Micaiah was of his calling beyond any shadow of doubt and that it was indeed the Spirit of God who spoke through him.

Because of the truth he proclaimed, Micaiah was put in prison with little food and water. This was Ahab's last act of defiance against God's messenger before he mounted his chariot to ride off to his own death.

Micaiah's life has left us with one of the brightest examples of what a true messenger of God must be like:

1. *He must be sure of his calling.*

2. *He must be committed from the beginning of his ministry to this one thing: "What my God says, that I will speak."* This absolute commitment to the message and to the One who sent him is the only way to endure and succeed under tremendous pressure and opposition.

3. *He must be willing to bear the consequences of his message, even if that means prison or death itself.*

I have a suggestion for you: Write Micaiah's commitment in your Bible on the front page: "As the LORD lives, what my God says, that I will speak." (2 Chronicles 18:13). Make it your commitment, and read it every time before you prepare a sermon or stand up to speak.

12

APPROVED
BY GOD

As believers and servants of God, we do not walk alone somewhere out in a desert doing our own thing. The Bible clearly says that we are part of a living body. Whatever we do will directly affect this living organism—the Body of Christ.

There are pastors, teachers and elders given to the church to help us with our walk and service to God. Their guidance, counsel and examples are vital to help us keep our focus and our faith pure.

However, in the midst of the most godly leadership and denominational traditions as well, we must never forget that ultimately we are responsible to God Himself. Our denomination or group may be satisfied with our activities, and they may approve of us and our ministry, but that is not enough. It must be God Himself who puts His stamp of approval on our lives and ministries.

The reason is this: He is the One who bought us with His precious blood. He is our owner and master, not a denomination or group! He directly called us to serve Him, not a system. And He also will be the judge of our lives and work!

PRESENT YOURSELF APPROVED TO GOD

The apostle Paul recognized that, even though he told those he had won to Christ to follow his example of faith, walk and service, he by no means was appointed to be their final judge. When he wrote to Timothy, one of the young preachers he personally discipled and trained, he said, "Be diligent to present yourself approved to God . . ." (2 Timothy 2:15).

Timothy was the closest "son" in the faith, co-worker, friend and disciple Paul had. I am convinced Timothy did all he could to please his older friend, spiritual father and teacher. But Paul was telling him: "Timothy, I am glad you please me with your love and service to the Lord. However, my approval of you is not enough. You must take your eyes off even me and present yourself approved to God."

With this attitude and command, Paul made Timothy directly responsible to God Himself.

I can easily imagine that Paul's evaluation and approval of Timothy would have been quite accurate. But Paul didn't take this authority upon himself. He knew exactly where the boundaries of his apostleship lay, and he was not about to take God's place.

This is an area in which Christianity has made grave mistakes. Systems and men-appointed leaders have become the final judge and source of approval for believers' lives, ministries and faith. No longer are they made directly responsible to God. Now, whatever the system or tradition prescribes has become the measurement of approval.

The problem with this is that many of these systems and traditions have slowly but steadily departed from the Bible. Suddenly, people are called on to choose the traditions of men and denominations rather than the commands of God.

This is exactly why Jesus got in trouble with the religious leadership of His time. He had to choose whether He was going to be approved by God, His Father, or by them. He chose to be approved of God, and this caused Him to be in constant conflict with the system in which He lived. It also was the reason, humanly speaking, for His persecution and His crucifixion.

There were some rulers who recognized that Jesus was indeed sent by God; however, they found it too difficult to choose to be approved by God instead of men. We read in John 12:42–43 about their decision: "Nevertheless many even of the rulers believed in Him, but because of the Pharisees they were not confessing Him, lest they should be put out of the synagogue; for they loved the approval of men rather than the approval of God."

Many of the heroes of the faith listed in Hebrews 11 were in the very same situation as Jesus. They had to make a decision whose approval they wanted to seek—man's or God's.

Noah and Abraham were lonely men in their generation, yet they presented themselves approved to God, by their faith (see Hebrews 11:1–2).

Joseph, after being sold into slavery, decided to present himself approved to God in the midst of a land of idolatry. As a servant and later as a prisoner in jail, he chose to keep God's command and suffer as an innocent man rather than to seek men's approval and lose God's.

Hebrews 11 also lists many **unknown martyrs** who chose to die rather than please men. What was their reward? God's approval of their faith and the promise of a reward in the future!

The same promise holds true for us as well. If we present ourselves approved to God, even if it costs a high price, there is a reward waiting for us: "Blessed is a man who perseveres under trial; for once he has been approved, he will receive the crown of life, which the Lord has promised to those who love Him" (James 1:12).

Great peace will come to our lives once we make up our

minds to seek God's approval alone, instead of the approval of others.

ONLY GOD'S EVALUATION IS PERFECT

We are often blessed to have very godly leaders and believers around us, who are a great help to us in getting our Christian lives "in shape" so that we are able to present ourselves approved to God.

But even the best of leaders and the most experienced pastors who know how to deal with people are not qualified to accurately judge someone's heart. Only God is able to do it. He made us, and nothing that is in our hearts is hidden before Him.

> For He knows the secrets of the heart (Psalm 44:21).

> The LORD knows the way of the righteous (Psalm 1:6).

> LORD, Thou hast searched me and known me. Thou dost know when I sit down and when I rise up; Thou dost understand my thought from afar. Thou dost scrutinize my path and my lying down, and art intimately acquainted with all my ways. Even before there is a word on my tongue, behold, O LORD, Thou dost know it all (Psalm 139:1-4).

As believers and Gospel workers, we must therefore willingly subject ourselves to the Lord's examination. His approval or disapproval of our lives and service is the only truly accurate assessment there is. It doesn't matter what we feel or think about ourselves or what others say about us. The only thing that counts for now and for all eternity is His approval of us and our ministry.

Paul addresses another problem in his second letter to the Corinthians: Gospel workers who approve of themselves and answer to no one. He points out what a trap and a deception this is.

For we are not bold to class or compare ourselves with some of those who commend themselves; but when they measure themselves by themselves, and compare themselves with themselves, they are without understanding. For not he who commends himself is approved, but whom the Lord commends (2 Corinthians 10:12, 18).

I believe this is a much-needed warning for the time in which we live, when many seem to be tempted to make a great name for themselves regardless of whether God approves them or not.

Encountering Disapproval and Accusations in Our Ministry

Making the mistake of seeking approval from men. As much as our call must come from the Lord Himself, our final approval must also come from Him alone. If we forget this, we will face much heartache and discouragement in our ministry.

As we serve the Lord, we seem to be continuously tempted to somehow seek the approval of men, especially those who are close to us or whose opinions are valued in our community or church. If the people we deal with would be like the apostle Paul, then it would be to our advantage to get their evaluation. Unfortunately, there are very few around with the heart of Paul.

Most of the time we encounter people who don't care if we sink or swim. There are those who will tell us anything we want to hear except the truth and others who are secretly jealous and criticize us no matter what we do. Finally, there are those who have made it their life's ambition to destroy us by spreading rumors, lies and false accusations. If we go around seeking men's approval, many years of our lives will be spent battling discouragement, bitterness and the desire to give it all up.

Disapproval from fellow believers. We have come to expect that the world hates us. We are not surprised or worried if they don't approve of our life and ministry.

But probably the most difficult things for us to handle are accusations and disapproval from fellow believers and other Christian workers. You see, the Body of Christ is supposed to be the most intimate family we have, and we expect to be loved, encouraged and supported in our efforts to build God's kingdom. However, at the same time, we often forget that God never asked us to seek the approval of our fellow Christians instead of Him.

I remember quite a number of years ago, as I was in our church, a lady stood up to give a nice testimony—and it bothered me. Just a few days earlier, word had come to me that she had told others that she didn't care for me at all. Because she knew of our ministry, I wondered why she wasn't at least careful with the things she said. While I was feeling bad about her attitude toward me, the Lord asked me there at church, "Why do you seek her approval?" I immediately realized that I felt bad because I had been seeking her approval of me instead of the Lord's!

Someone who really got in trouble by seeking men's approval was Joseph. Joseph was 17 years old when God started to speak to him through dreams. He related these dreams to his brothers, hoping for their approval, understanding and joy over God speaking to him. After all, they were not outsiders. As his own family, they were closest to him. They were the sons of Israel and heirs of Abraham's blessings. Wasn't it safe to seek their approval?

With his expectations, Joseph earned their jealousy and hatred and was sold as a slave to Egypt. You see, the problem was that these sons of Israel were still very much in the making. God had two decades of work to do in their hearts before they were mature enough to meet Joseph again and accept the interpretation of those dreams.

Why might our fellow believers not approve of us? Surely there will be brothers and sisters in the Body of Christ who will do all they can to encourage us in our ministry and in the vision God has given us for our lives. However, there will be others who will not approve of us; here are some reasons why:

1. *The believers we deal with might not have the maturity, insight or vision to be able to understand why we make certain decisions.* They may not be able to comprehend why we invest our lives in things for which they have no burden.

2. *We may give cause for confusion.* We make mistakes out of lack of experience, and we make unfortunate decisions we have to reverse later. We are not always correct in our perceptions, nor do we always act wisely in what we say, how we say it and to whom.

3. *Some believers and Gospel workers feel threatened by our success.* If we do well in our ministry, they feel overlooked, left out and put down. Unless a person is very careful, he will give room for jealousy and open his heart to any suggestions the devil might have.

It takes great maturity and love for the kingdom of God to be selfless in the sight of others' "glory." John the Baptist was such a man. He lost his audience, his disciples and his popularity to Jesus, but he stood there rejoicing and saying, "He must increase, but I must decrease" (John 3:30).

4. *The person who does not approve of us is a carnal Christian who has left Jesus' command to "love one another."* He has given room to envy and every imagination originating from the devil's inspiration. If such a person continues in his way, he will be so deceived that he will think it is his right and his duty to go against his brother. In his heart he has not only accused him, but already convicted and sentenced him. Now he is on a crusade to justify and prove that his judgment was right. He is so deceived that he cannot see or recognize his deception.

How to deal with accusations and disapproval. It doesn't really matter whether the accusations and disapproval come from people who hate us because they don't know the Lord, from believers who are genuinely concerned or from others who are jealous. What matters is what we are going to do about it.

We could fight back with the same bitterness, or we could perhaps take legal action. We could defend ourselves and prove to everyone how right we are. We could set out to take revenge, or we could walk away from everything, disillusioned and brokenhearted.

As believers and servants of the King of kings, we must find the humility of heart to reflect our Heavenly Father and to approach the situation as Jesus would.

1. We should take the whole matter to the Lord and ask for His wisdom for each situation.

2. If the person who accuses us is right in his accusation, we must change and correct what we did wrong. Our hearts must be sensitive enough to accept correction, even from an enemy if he is right.

3. If our conscience is clear and the accusations are unfounded, we must go on serving the Lord without being worried, bitter or troubled. We are called upon to forgive as Jesus would and to leave our burdens with Him. He is able to deal with those who disapprove of us unjustly. We do not have to justify ourselves. He will do it on our behalf, in His own time and in His own way. All we must do is to keep our hearts clear toward God and toward those who disapprove of us.

4. As for us, we are called on to have peace with all men—if possible (see Romans 12:18). Let us be willing to take steps toward this peace, especially if it involves other believers. A face-to-face talk (not fight), a word spoken in humility, deliberately praying and blessing our "enemy," choosing not to reply to angry words, waiting patiently for God to defend us—all these things are biblical avenues to help bring about this peace.

We should focus on our own hearts. We can end up being so hurt and so discouraged that our service to the Lord may become less than effective.

I have learned a lot from my husband in this area by watching how he has dealt with people who thought they were so justified in their accusations toward him. At the time when he first came to the United States to go to Bible school and especially after our marriage, some of his former co-workers, leaders and friends thought he had left the faith and forgotten his commitment to the Lord, his burden for India and the lost world.

I remember well how stunned I was by some of the letters he received, and I asked him what he was going to do about it. He said, "Nothing. These people are disappointed or have hurt feelings. I cannot prove to them that I am right. Give it time and God will show it to them." He never replied to the accusations by defending himself. All he did was thank them for their love and concern.

After a few years, some of these same brothers wrote and asked for forgiveness. Today they are our very best friends in the ministry.

In our ministry we receive all sorts of letters, from all kinds of people. Some are wonderful, but a few accuse us of things we have never said, done or even thought about. Sometimes I wonder what great bitterness must have caused these people to say all these things. It used to hurt my feelings when I read some of these accusations, because I know my husband's heart and his burden for the lost. If they could only see his life, the endless travels, the little time he can spend at home, the burdens of leading a ministry and the hours early in the morning and late at night when he studies and prepares his daily radio broadcasts, besides everything else. I often wish those people would take a look at his life and his heart before judging something they don't even know about.

But recently I found a way to look at those letters in a different light; and I must say, they don't bother me much anymore. The Lord reminded me of something He Himself said in

Matthew 10:24–25: "A disciple is not above his teacher, nor a slave above his master. If they have called the head of the house Beelzebul, how much more the members of his household!"

Do you know what that means? The religious leaders not only disapproved of Jesus being the Messiah, but they actually declared that He was possessed not just by a demon but by Satan himself. After you are accused of this, there is nothing else left of which to be accused!

Jesus said that if He faced this kind of treatment, we can be sure that we will face the very same thing! For us, this means that by the time our lives are over, we should have been accused of everything! It should be no surprise to us when people accuse us of anything they can think of. We should actually expect it to happen. No matter how careful we are, we must remember that if Jesus, who never did anything wrong, ended up with such severe accusations, we will too.

The Bible tells us that none of us should give any cause to be accused rightly, but that we must live in such a way that when things are checked out, our accusers will be proved wrong:

> Keep a good conscience so that in the thing in which you are slandered, those who revile your good behavior in Christ may be put to shame. For it is better, if God should will it so, that you suffer for doing what is right rather than for doing what is wrong (1 Peter 3:16–17).

> By no means let any of you suffer as a murderer, or thief, or evildoer, or a troublesome meddler (1 Peter 4:15).

There is even a special blessing promised to those who face false accusations because of Christ:

> Blessed are you when men revile you, and persecute you, and say all kinds of evil against you falsely, on account of Me. Rejoice and be glad, for your reward in heaven is great, for so

they persecuted the prophets who were before you (Matthew 5:11–12).

If you are reviled for the name of Christ, you are blessed, because the Spirit of glory and of God rests upon you. But if anyone suffers as a Christian, let him not feel ashamed, but in that name let him glorify God (1 Peter 4:14, 16).

Whatever happens around us, let us walk before our God with a pure heart, seeking His approval alone. Men's accusations and disapproval will come and go. We must determine that they will never become the reason for us to look back after we have put our hands to the plow.

CARING
FOR
GOD'S
Children

> > > > >

As you are called to serve the living God, either full-time or within your local church, you will inevitably deal with the lives and souls of other people. When you read the Scripture, Old or New Testament, many times you will see the concern and grief of God the Father over the treatment His people received from those who were supposed to shepherd, lead, protect and teach them.

James and Paul wrote:

Let not many of you become teachers, my brethren, knowing
that as such we shall incur a stricter judgment (James 3:1).

And let these also first be tested; then let them serve as deacons if they are beyond reproach (1 Timothy 3:10).

The apostles wrote these instructions because they were very
much aware of what a serious thing it is to take care of God's
own children. They are the apple of His eye, regardless of how
insignificant they might look.

If you are called to be a caretaker of His children, you had
better be aware of this: Whatever you do with them, good or
bad, God will demand an account from you for each of them
(see Hebrews 13:17).

God has a purpose for each individual believer in His kingdom, and your duty is to get them ready for it. It takes a tremendous amount of patience, prayer, teaching, love and wisdom to
accomplish this. Bringing up God's own sons and daughters is
an enormous task that you should go about with fear and trembling, not with an attitude of arrogance or negligence.

To better understand what God expects from us, let us divide this task into three major areas: feeding His sheep, making
disciples and completion in Christ.

➤ ➤ ➤ ➤ ➤

13

FEED MY SHEEP

esus commissioned Peter three times to feed His sheep or lambs (John 21:15–17, KJV).

I suppose that Jesus had many reasons to reaffirm His love and His calling to Peter after he had denied Him three times. But perhaps Jesus knew that Peter had the tendency to forget what the primary task of a true shepherd was: feeding the sheep. This means taking them to places where they find enough grass and water not only to sustain their lives, but also to look healthy and develop normally.

Jesus was very concerned that Peter would not only lead the sheep, protect them and increase the flock, but that he actually would give them food to eat as well. This sounds so simple and logical that we might wonder why Jesus put such an emphasis on it. I believe He did it because He knew that Peter, and many of the shepherds after him, would continually be tempted to get involved in other important issues and in the process forget to feed the sheep.

WHAT DO I FEED THE SHEEP?

Jesus was well aware that man was created as a spirit being, and as such he must have spiritual food to survive. The devil, however, very cleverly offered Jesus (and he offers us as well) physical bread for our spiritual hunger. Jesus immediately recognized that this substitute, however tempting it might appear, could never satisfy or nourish His Spirit. Because of this, He rejected the devil's offer, and He very clearly stated the reason why: "Man shall not live on bread alone, but on every word that proceeds out of the mouth of God" (Matthew 4:4).

Man always looks and searches to find something to feed his spirit. God has told us that His Word is the only food by which we can live. He has not only told us what we need, but He has provided it and sent it directly from heaven. The apostle John describes it with these words: "In the beginning was the Word, and the Word was with God, and the Word was God. And the Word became flesh" (John 1:1, 14).

Jesus knew that He was this Word and, therefore, the very food mankind would need. Without fear, He declared this to those who listened to His teaching. We read His words in John 6:

> It is not Moses who has given you the bread out of heaven, but it is My Father who gives you the true bread out of heaven (v. 32).

> For the bread of God is that which comes down out of heaven, and gives life to the world (v. 33).

> I am the bread of life; he who comes to Me shall not hunger, and he who believes in Me shall never thirst (v. 35).

> I am the living bread that came down out of heaven; if any one eats of this bread, he shall live forever; and the bread also which I shall give for the life of the world is My flesh (v. 51).

> Truly, truly, I say to you, unless you eat the flesh of the Son of Man and drink His blood, you have no life in yourselves. He who eats My flesh and drinks My blood has eternal life; and I will raise him up on the last day. For My flesh is true food,

and My blood is true drink. He who eats My flesh and drinks
My blood abides in Me, and I in him. As the living Father
sent Me, and I live because of the Father, so he who eats Me,
he also shall live because of Me. This is the bread which came
down out of heaven; not as the fathers ate, and died, he who
eats this bread shall live forever (vv. 53–58).

Jesus possibly offended more people with this declaration
than with anything else He said. In the first place, it sounded
too radical, cannibalistic and exclusive. His audience walked
off, not wanting to hear any further explanation or interpretation. They were ready to take some of Jesus with which they
could feed their spirits, but not all of Him. They still wanted
their spiritual diets to have more variety, perhaps adding some
traditions, some philosophies of the Pharisees and some favorite man-made interpretations of the Scriptures.

It was too hard for these Jews to accept the fact that Jesus
Himself was the only thing they needed for their salvation and
their spiritual food. They did not recognize that Jesus was the
full revelation and incarnation of the Word of God. Nothing
was missing.

What do all these Bible verses mean for us today? If a shepherd decides to feed his flock with anything less or more than
the whole Word of God, he is about to kill his sheep! At the
very least, he will weaken their health and make them vulner-
able to disease.

Does this mean that we cannot talk about anything else, such
as church history, human relationships or health issues, in our
churches? No, I don't mean this at all. Some of these things are
very important for our lives here on earth, as well as our better understanding of the Bible. However, if we attempt to feed people's
spirits with doctrinal debates, denominational pride, church poli-
tics, upholding of traditions, political issues, pet doctrines and so
on, it will not do one thing for their spiritual health.

It is the Word, and the Word alone, that brings conviction of sin, salvation, freedom, healing and deliverance.

> "Is not My word like *fire?*" declares the LORD, "and like a *hammer* which shatters a rock?" (Jeremiah 23:29).

> Therefore every one who hears these words of Mine, and acts upon them, may be compared to a wise man, who built his house upon the *rock* (Matthew 7:24).

> For the word of God is living and active and sharper than any two-edged *sword*, and piercing as far as the division of soul and spirit, of both joints and marrow, and able to judge the thoughts and intentions of the heart (Hebrews 4:12).

> He sent His word and *healed* them (Psalm 107:20).

> So shall My word be which goes forth from My mouth; it shall not return to Me empty, *without accomplishing what I desire*, and without succeeding in the matter for which I sent it (Isaiah 55:11).

> Heaven and earth will pass away, but My words *shall not pass away* (Matthew 24:35).

> The sum of Thy word is *truth* (Psalm 119:160).

> And you shall know the truth, and the truth shall *make you free* (John 8:32).

The apostle Paul, who was more educated than most of his contemporaries and definitely more than the rest of the apostles, made this statement about his own ministry: "For I determined to know nothing among you except Jesus Christ, and Him crucified" (1 Corinthians 2:2).

With this, he testified fully to the fact that no matter how wonderful and great a philosophy or tradition or how brilliant a human idea may be, it can never do in a thousand years what the Word of God can do in one single moment.

How Healthy Are the Sheep?

If we want to determine whether a shepherd feeds his sheep or not, we only need to observe how healthy his sheep look and act. It is amazing how many shepherds think they feed their sheep, when they actually beat them every time they come to church instead. It doesn't seem to matter how wounded, how discouraged or how hungry the sheep are, they still hear a condemnation sermon each time they show up. Thus they go home feeling even more terrible than when they came.

There is definitely a place for correction and discipline, but when it is out of proportion, it will fail to achieve God's purpose. Only when a sheep is well fed by his shepherd will he or she develop an inner trust to accept correction and positively benefit from it.

In some fellowships, the sheep are given starvation rations—not enough to really thrive on but just a little too much to die. God's original intention was to have a Church that is a powerful witness on earth, invincible and well able to face the attacks of the devil. However, this is impossible if the shepherd is feeding his sheep too little of the truth or not often enough.

Perhaps the reason may be that within the framework of a denomination, the shepherd has been denied the liberty to go beyond denominational beliefs with his teaching. The reason could also be that the shepherd lacks understanding of the Word of God and of the need of his flock, or he may not prepare himself well through prayer, study and a personal commitment to God to preach the truth regardless of man-made restrictions.

Then in other places, the diet of the sheep consists of only one type of "grass," and the sheep suffer from severe malnutrition due to lack of essential nutrients.

Jesus said that we live on *every* word that proceeds out of the mouth of God. This means that we are not meant to live by only one or two words, but by every one of God's words. Unless the whole counsel of God is proclaimed and taught, we are not able to function normally.

For example, believers who hear only about grace and love will not know how to do spiritual warfare or evangelism, and the world around them will go to hell. If all that is taught consists of waiting for the second coming of Christ, the church will miss the chance to be salt and light in its generation.

We must not worry that the sheep entrusted to us will be at a disadvantage if we don't have a college degree or doctorate or if we know little about human philosophies. As long as we are faithful in giving them the Word of God, they will receive the best food available for their spirits.

PREPARATION OF THE FOOD

Whether you hold the office of a pastor or if you disciple only one convert, your primary goal must always be to feed your sheep in the best way possible. You cannot expect to do justice to the task and come up with a well-balanced meal for your sheep if you hope that God will just drop the message in your heart the moment you stand up to preach. Neither should you be a bit surprised to find your teaching shallow if you glance through your Bible to find something to talk about five minutes before Sunday school starts.

Some people believe that no preparation, and especially no notes, is a clear sign of being led by the Holy Spirit. They have seen great men of God stand before a huge crowd and preach for three hours without notes and with great anointing.

We must not be mistaken. The anointing and the wisdom of these men are *not* rooted in the absence of notes or preparation, but rather in a lifelong walk with the Lord. Many of them have years of experience as pastors and evangelists, and they have lived, studied, taught and prayed for years through the Scriptures they teach.

There are pastors who can not only recite entire chapters by heart, but who can talk on almost any subject, references included, without opening their Bibles. This looks very impressive; but believe me, these abilities didn't come cheaply to them or without study. The truth is, they have worked and studied harder than others in order to qualify to teach, preach and counsel.

There is no doubt that God is able to give instant messages or a revelation of Scripture, but we must not try to assume that these moments of special grace are the only thing needed to feed the sheep. When we look in the Bible, we find that God expects those who lead others to know the Scriptures through diligent study, prayer and application in their own lives.

This is what God commanded—and expects of—those He has appointed as leaders and teachers:

> This book of the law shall not depart from your mouth, but you shall meditate on it day and night, so that you may be careful to do according to all that is written in it; for then you will make your way prosperous, and then you will have success (Joshua 1:8).

> Pay close attention to yourself and to your teaching; persevere in these things; for as you do this you will insure salvation both for yourself and for those who hear you (1 Timothy 4:16).

> Study to shew thyself approved unto God, a workman that needeth not to be ashamed, rightly dividing the word of truth (2 Timothy 2:15, KJV).

From childhood you have known the sacred writings which are able to give you the wisdom. . . . All Scripture is inspired by God and profitable for teaching, for reproof, for correction, for training in righteousness; that the man of God may be adequate, equipped for every good work (2 Timothy 3:15–17).

Preach the word; be ready in season and out of season; reprove, rebuke, exhort, with great patience and instruction (2 Timothy 4:2).

For the overseer must be above reproach as God's steward, . . . holding fast the faithful word which is in accordance with the teaching, that he may be able both to exhort in sound doctrine and to refute those who contradict (Titus 1:7, 9).

It takes a tremendous amount of time, discipline and commitment not only to qualify to become a shepherd, but to correctly feed the sheep as well.

If you teach others, you must first set a specific goal of what you want them to learn. Then, you must make careful plans as to how to bring them from where they are now to that goal.

Paul was not a "hit-and-miss" preacher. Whenever he stood up to preach and teach his converts, he knew exactly what his goal was. He tells us this in 1 Timothy 1:5: "But the *goal* of our instruction is love from a pure heart and a good conscience and a sincere faith."

No single truth of the Bible is meant to stand alone without it being further explained, balanced, completed and put in proper perspective by the whole of Scripture. Therefore, it is our obligation to feed the sheep by teaching the *entire* Scripture in a well-planned manner. It has to be done with the leading of the Holy Spirit, step-by-step, and in a very practical way that enables your people to apply what they have learned to their everyday lives.

Many of your converts will come from non-Christian or nominal Christian backgrounds and will need special instruction in foundational doctrines, major biblical events and basic Christian living and values. You need to have a teaching series tailor-made just for them and special classes set up to help them gain understanding and get the right start. The class must be separate from the regular church service to give them the opportunity to ask questions.

In your normal church service, you must have the goal to teach your people systematically. This is not done by only speaking on various topics or Bible stories or by picking verses out at random from the Bible. These methods all have their rightful place and purpose. But systematically instructing them in the Word of God requires that you teach book by book and verse by verse through the entire Bible. Remember: "Man shall not live on bread alone, but on *every* word that proceeds out of the mouth of God" (Matthew 4:4).

Unless your people are taught the entire Word linked together, they will not become spiritually strong and immovable in their faith. They will have bits and pieces of truth floating around in their heads, not knowing how they belong together. What they need is to be grounded and established in the Word and in their faith, which will only happen when the entire Scripture becomes part of their lives.

To teach systematically might require a change in the traditional format of your service. Unless you have set aside a specific time for this teaching, it will not work.

Many times in our Indian church services, there are four or five visiting preachers waiting to get a chance to speak. Some of them will preach for two hours without a break, and only very few abide by the time reserved for them. If you plan to do your teaching after your people have already listened to five sermons, you can forget it. The human mind is only capable of so much concentration and input.

If you cannot restrict guest speakers from using up the entire service, you should do your teaching first, right after the worship. You must be more concerned that your sheep are fed right rather than trying to please guest speakers at the expense of the sheep's welfare.

BEING GOOD STEWARDS OF THE WORD

God is with us in every step as we go about feeding His sheep. He hasn't left us alone with this enormous task, but He has given us the Holy Spirit to enlighten and instruct us how to break the Bread of Life. At the same time, He works in every believer, opening their understanding and leading them into all truth.

I am sure that as you prepare to feed your sheep, the Holy Spirit gives you ideas, insights and understanding of how Scripture connects together. And often as you speak, powerful examples come to your mind and you are able to use them effectively. Other times, while you ride in a bus, work in the kitchen or walk down the road, God opens up His Word to you.

What do you do with all this insight? I'll tell you what the devil does with it: He works very hard to rob and to steal it!

Because of our human limitations, we can only remember so much. After two hours or two days of busy work, we can only retain a fraction of the good thoughts we had last week.

Dear brother, dear sister—how can it benefit you in your ministry today if you had 15 good illustrations in the past three weeks on how to present a specific truth, but you forgot 14 of them?

I firmly believe that the Holy Spirit expects us to be good stewards, not only of our possessions, but especially of the truth He reveals to us and the insights He gives us into Scripture. God expects us to work with what He has entrusted to us. There is no doubt that He knows our limitations and how much we are able to remember. However, most of us have no excuse because He has given us the ability to write things down.

Perhaps you feel that you don't have any talent to write or even spell things very well. This doesn't matter at all. Your notes are just for you, to help you remember the things God has taught you. As long as you can read them, they are enough.

Just to give you a few ideas, let me share some things with you that have worked for me.

I always keep a notebook and a pen with me. This notebook is not for writing sermons and outlines. It is a collection of small thoughts, ideas, an understanding of a truth or an illustration. There is no particular order to it. I just use it whenever I feel that God has given me something I don't want to forget.

Often, these notes are just a few words or a sentence or two. However, I later use these collections of thoughts when I prepare for a message or teaching. In fact, quite a number of the subjects in this book started with just a small entry in my notebook.

If I prepare a teaching for a ladies' meeting, for example, *I not only make a short outline with the major points, but I write a second one with every thought written out* in such a way that I can pick up my notes after three years and know exactly what I meant at that time.

Often I only take the short outline to my meeting, because the content is so fresh in my heart. However, I know from experience that if I don't speak on the same subject for a year or more, the thoughts I once had will be lost and buried under a thousand other ones—unless I write them down and keep them in my file.

After speaking in a meeting, I correct my teaching notes. During the presentation I discover whether some parts might be too long, lack enough illustrations or be irrelevant to people's life-styles. Many times as I speak, good thoughts and examples I had not thought of before come to my mind. If I don't add them to my notes right away, they will get lost.

You need to find your own ways of preserving what God gives to you. It is your responsibility, and all it takes is just a little discipline!

14

MAKING DISCIPLES

*M*aking disciples is probably the most joyful, as well as the most fearful, part of the process for anyone whom the Lord has called to care for His children. Disciples are not born; they are made!

A new Christian is no different from a newborn baby. He has the breath of life in him, but he doesn't know how to live in this world! The ones who nurture him will undoubtedly become his models for language, actions, work, love, affection, right and wrong, commitment, endurance, faithfulness and obedience.

It is not enough to tell a small child, "Feed yourself, dress yourself, and learn your ABCs." No, you must patiently show him how and assist him until he finally learns even the most basic of tasks.

In the same way, it is not enough to tell your new converts, "This is what the Bible says on this subject—now go and do it." No, you must *live* the truth you try to teach them in such a clear way that you can confidently say: "Watch me; this is how it looks practically, and this is the way you can live it too."

Jesus "made" His disciples by portraying everything He taught in front of their eyes. The Pharisees interpreted Scripture to the people with their philosophies and debates, but Jesus interpreted Scripture by living it. There was no discrepancy between His words and deeds. When He called His disciples with the words "Follow Me," it meant more than just traveling with Him through the countryside. It meant this: "Imitate Me, learn by observing Me, and then do exactly as you saw Me do it."

Paul never said this to the Christians he had won: "You read the Scripture and then figure out how to apply it." No, he actually encouraged them to imitate him and to learn by watching, just as Jesus did.

Paul didn't think of himself as perfect, but he recognized his responsibility as an apostle and teacher. He knew these converts had never seen Jesus walking on the earth. He knew they had never met Peter, John or James personally. In fact, most of them were from heathen backgrounds, having no clue about the law of Moses and the God of Israel. If Paul had not practically shown them how to live out their new faith, they would not have had any model for their lives.

You can make believers with the right teachings, but you cannot make disciples without being a living example.

Before Jesus went to heaven, He commanded His followers to make disciples of all nations. In other words, He told them: "You became My disciples by watching Me; now you must go and make disciples by letting others watch you."

When we recognize this principle, it puts a tremendous pressure and responsibility on us to walk, talk, think and act in a manner that is worthy of Jesus and worthy to be imitated. You see, it is not our words or teaching that qualify us to make disciples. It is our everyday lives, our private innermost thoughts, our dealing with others, our relationships with our wife or husband or children. If we want to make disciples, we cannot have thoughts and actions that contradict the Word of God. We have to be real to the core.

The Body of Christ is hurting very deeply in this area. It

seems that so many believers who are supposed to be mature—elders and even pastors—disqualify themselves by holding on to grudges, gossip, greed, unforgiveness and revenge. When confronted, they defend and justify their actions and motives.

What kind of disciples do you make? You will reproduce exactly what you are yourself. Even your secret attitudes will show up in your disciples. This is simply the law of seed and harvest. The seed you sow into your disciples will produce accordingly.

Paul was very much aware of the fact that, unless the leadership in the Body of Christ portrays the character of Jesus, the whole church will be in trouble. Therefore, he wrote very clear guidelines in 1 and 2 Timothy and in Titus for those who are in any kind of leadership. Elders, deacons and pastors are required to have a life, private or public, that is beyond reproach. Their wives and families as well must be examples that are worthy to be followed.

You—as a leader, pastor, Sunday school teacher, Bible woman or missionary—set the atmosphere and the standard for your group, fellowship, ministry or church. You will see exactly what you are yourself reproduced in others. If you are critical, negative and argumentative, you will end up with disciples who are just like that.

It is actually very simple: If you want loving people—you must portray love. If you desire giving people—you must practice giving. If you want forgiving people—you must extend forgiveness. If you long to have people of faith—you must exercise faith. And remember, you cannot stop at showing these godly characteristics only once. You must portray them again and again before your people, until they learn it.

It is an awesome responsibility before God to shape the lives of other people with the example of our own lives. In addition to this, whatever they have learned by observing us, they will pass on to the next generation of believers!

Often, when a pastor takes over an existing church, he finds himself surrounded by disciples who display very un-Christlike traits such as selfishness and pride. Someone in the previous leadership of that church must have portrayed that character trait before them, or at least tolerated it when it entered the church door. It is a terrible task, and nearly impossible, for a pastor to rid a church of such un-Christlike characteristics, especially if they became traditions long ago and have been passed along by several generations of believers.

In many ways, I hope and pray that you will be extremely cautious from the very beginning of your ministry, because what you live before your people will determine the kind of disciples you make.

15

COMPLETE IN
CHRIST

*W*hen God asked us to feed His sheep and to make disciples out of them, He had one single goal in mind: that one day each of His sheep will attain a maturity as described in Ephesians 4:11–13:

> And He gave some as apostles, and some as prophets, and some as evangelists, and some as pastors and teachers, for the equipping of the saints for the work of service, to the building up of the body of Christ; until we all attain to the unity of the faith, and of the knowledge of the Son of God, to a mature man, to the measure of the stature which belongs to the fullness of Christ.

Unless we as Gospel workers keep God's perspective and final goal for His sheep before our eyes at all times, we will get lost, taking them in a thousand different directions, and end up with a flock of 40-year-old baby sheep.

In order for a newborn child to become a mature adult, he or she must naturally go through several different developmental stages. Each new level builds on the growth and skills acquired during the previous months and years of training. However, the parents know well that for normal development, there is a definite time limit to each stage. The whole process of growing up should be completed within a reasonable number of years.

Exactly what we see taking place in the physical development of a child from birth to maturity *must also* take place in the spiritual development of each person born into the family of God. God has made it easy for us as "spiritual parents" to understand and to know what normal spiritual growth looks like. He has given us the physical pattern of a child's development to observe and to go by, as we care for and train the spiritual children God has given us.

To make it simple, we will divide the growing-up period into three major stages and look at each one from a physical as well as a spiritual standpoint, in the light of Ephesians 4:11–13.

STAGE ONE: TOTAL DEPENDENCE

The birth of a new baby usually brings joy to the whole family. There is an atmosphere of excitement and celebration when you enter the house. Grandma and Grandpa, as well as all the rest of the relatives, come to visit.

But the most obvious change of all is that for a long time after the baby is born, the parents and other helpers are busier than at any other time in this baby's life. At this point, the newborn baby is in a stage of total dependency on others. He cannot even hold his head up by himself. Someone has to attend to every one of his needs. He must be held, comforted, fed, burped, clothed, cleaned, bathed and carried from one place to another. So, while the baby is a great joy to have in the family, he requires continuous attention and special care.

Paul talks about this same experience when he describes how he took care of his new converts:

> I gave you milk to drink, not solid food; for you were not yet
> able to receive it (1 Corinthians 3:2).

But we proved to be gentle among you, as a nursing mother tenderly cares for her own children (1 Thessalonians 2:7).

Therefore be on the alert, remembering that night and day for a period of three years I did not cease to admonish each one with tears (Acts 20:31).

In Ephesians 4:11-13, Paul tells us that God gave apostles, prophets, evangelists, pastors and teachers for the purpose of (1) equipping the saints and (2) building up the Body of Christ. In other words, God did not leave the care and upbringing of His newborn children to chance! On the contrary, He planned it very carefully, by assigning the job of father, mother and nurse-maid to His most qualified servants!

Why did He do this? We often think that the most qualified teachers and leaders should look after the most advanced believers, because almost anybody can take care of the new converts. Perhaps we should ask ourselves this question: Who in all the church needs the most building up? Is it not the new converts?

But before any building up can be done, something else needs to happen first, which in my opinion is the main reason why God has selected such a special task force to attend to the new believers. In this stage of total dependency, as well as in the next stage, the most crucial event in the life of a believer *must* take place: the laying of the foundation of his faith and walk with God.

This foundation has to be laid by someone who really knows what he is doing, because it must be strong enough to withstand every storm of life and every attack of Satan and his demon forces. Even though the whole church will—and must—be involved in bringing up the new family member, the responsibility of laying the foundation and watching over the building process must be carried out by those whom the Lord has specifically appointed and equipped for this task.

Paul wrote about this in 1 Corinthians 3:10: "According to the grace of God which was given to me, as a wise master builder I laid a foundation, and another is building upon it. But let each man be careful how he builds upon it."

STAGE TWO: DOING THINGS FOR HIMSELF

Now the baby is getting older. He is gaining strength, and he begins to observe and imitate others. He can hold up his head by himself, and before long he turns over, sits up, crawls, stands and eventually walks without any help. He learns to grasp things with his fingers and soon is able to perform simple tasks.

Very early on he makes sounds that develop into words and later into complete sentences. As the child grows a little older, he learns to eat by himself. Of course, as he starts out, he will spill a lot of rice and make a big mess. However, some of the food will end up in his mouth, and before long the child is able to feed himself.

This is a stage of new discoveries for the child, as well as many dangers. The child is curious and tries out his newly acquired skills. He climbs on chairs and tables, tries to touch the fire and stuffs hazardous objects in his mouth.

The child needs constant supervision, guidance, protection and correction because he is not yet able to recognize dangers. However, with time, practice and the right guidance, he learns to walk, talk and feed himself without any help.

Spiritually, during this second stage, a new Christian grows from a totally dependent baby Christian into a child of God who has learned the basic skills of walking in his new faith, talking with God through prayer and feeding himself with the Word of God by reading and consistently practicing the Scriptures.

At this second stage, the main work of the "building up" team is to encourage and stimulate every new attempt to learn a skill. It is vital to provide clear direction as well as loving correction and protection. A wise and experienced teacher will take into consideration the growth rate and ability to learn of each individual child of God. This is important because if pushed too hard or too early or not encouraged enough, the young believer will either get hurt or experience a standstill.

That is why Paul instructs Timothy in 1 Timothy 3:6 not to put a new convert in charge of a church. This is not because the new believer doesn't love God enough or has no zeal to serve Him. He probably has more enthusiasm than most older believers. However, Paul wants the new convert to first have enough time to develop his personal relationship with God, pass a few tests, gain experience in battle, learn humility and be proven in his faith and commitment.

The whole factor Paul emphasizes here is this: Development and maturity do not happen instantly; rather, they take time. We have to grant this time to a believer if we don't want to endanger him or allow the church to get hurt.

However, at the end of this second stage, with the right instructions, building up and encouragement, the young believer will have successfully learned the basic skills for his personal walk with God.

Stage Three: Doing Things for Others

When parents teach and bring up their son and daughter, they do it with a specific expectation. They desire that later on their children will have reached a maturity level at which they not only can do things for themselves, but for others as well.

You expect your daughter to iron the clothes and cook for the family. You expect your son to go to the rice fields and help with the farm work. After all, they are now old enough to take on some responsibility.

When we read the passage in Ephesians 4:11-15 very carefully, we can see clearly that these pastors, teachers and others are not given to the believers for an unlimited time, but only *until* they have reached maturity (v. 13). They are expected by God Himself to grow up:

> To a *mature man*, to the measure of the stature which belongs to the fullness of Christ (v. 13)

> To no longer be children (v. 14)

> In all aspects into Him (v. 15)

In other words, for every believer there must come a time in his life when the parents are no longer needed and his training is complete. The kind of maturity that God expects from each believer is to be equipped "for the work of service" (v. 12). This means when you as Gospel worker did your job right, your converts must be able to do ministry as well—on their own. Remember, you are given to them *until* maturity.

Jesus had His disciples with Him. Throughout the four Gospels we read how He trained them, always knowing that He had only three years until the cross. By then His training and teaching would be cut off, whether they were ready or not.

However, Jesus planned ahead. One day He called them and basically told them, "Now you have watched Me long enough and you have heard enough teaching. You have reached a level of maturity where I can send you to do the 'work of service.' " Jesus clearly outlined what He meant by this in Matthew 10:7–8: "And as you go, preach, saying, 'The kingdom of heaven is at hand.' Heal the sick, raise the dead, cleanse the lepers, cast out demons; freely you received, freely give."

To recognize that this is what Jesus calls "the work of service" might cause a pastor or elder to ask: "Lord, are you sure that I am supposed to train each of my converts to have such faith and courage to do all these things? Is it not enough for them if I teach them to sing, collect the offering and once in a while pass out a Gospel tract? Shouldn't it be someone else's job to go after these other more difficult tasks?"

I believe this attitude has made many of our churches very weak.

Many believers expect their pastor to hold their hands, weep with them and be there for them whenever they need comfort, healing or an answer to prayer. He is the one who is supposed to touch heaven for them and do warfare on their behalf. After all, he is the pastor, and they are only poor sheep.

Biblically, this is totally wrong. When we read the book of Acts, we see a powerful church in which "the work of service" was not limited to one or two people but was shared by all believers.

In Mark 16:16-18, Jesus declared that *"those who have believed"* will cast out demons and heal the sick. He didn't limit this activity to those whom He appointed as pastors, elders or missionaries. According to this Scripture alone, God obviously expects more from an "ordinary" believer than just passing out songbooks.

Our responsibility must be to teach *every* believer how to do spiritual warfare, because there is a village, a nation and a world to be won for Christ. It is impossible for the pastor to do it all by himself. In God's plan, the devil should have reason to tremble before even a little grandmother in our congregation because she is about "the work of service."

After the resurrection, Jesus told His disciples, "As the Father has sent Me, I also send you" (John 20:21). This means that we and the believers entrusted to us are now called to do exactly what Jesus Himself used to do: "The Spirit of the Lord is upon Me, because He anointed Me to preach the gospel to the poor. He has sent Me to proclaim release to the captives, and recovery of sight to the blind, to set free those who are downtrodden, to proclaim the favorable year of the Lord" (Luke 4:18-19).

Furthermore, Jesus explained to His disciples the kind of attitude He had while performing His ministry and that He expected them to have the same: "It is not so among you, but whoever wishes to become great among you shall be your servant, and whoever wishes to be first among you shall be your slave; just as the Son of Man did not come to be served, but to serve, and to give His life a ransom for many" (Matthew 20:26–28).

Last, He commissioned His disciples to go into all the world and make disciples of all nations. He charged them also with these words: ". . . teaching them to observe *all* that I commanded you" (Matthew 28:20).

What does all this mean? As responsible Gospel workers, we cannot afford to teach our converts less than what God expects of them. We must seek with all diligence to bring them to a maturity level at which they are useful for God's kingdom and qualified to do the work of the ministry.

MATURITY PROBLEMS

Whenever growing up takes place, physically or spiritually, things do not always go smoothly. Parents and children encounter maturity problems that need to be solved before the desired goal can be reached. Let us deal here with just two of these problems.

The child's problem. Most children are excited to grow up and begin to earn adult privileges, such as staying up late, going places, making decisions, spending money, buying nice clothes and so on. Yet often these same children don't want to take on adult responsibilities.

The daughter finds it easier if Mommy does all the cooking, ironing and cleaning, because she is much faster and better. The daughter has reached a maturity level to master these skills, and with practice she could increase her speed and ability as well, but she would still rather have others serve her.

The son is now able to carry heavy loads and work in the field for his father, but he doesn't want to do it. When the son was little, Daddy did all this hard work and the little boy only watched him. But now the son is taller than his father, and he has big shoulders too! However, he still prefers to let his father do the field work, because Daddy has always done it anyway. After all, life is more comfortable if he can avoid being exhausted by hard work.

Many times a pastor faces the same kind of problems in his church. There are mature, "grown up" believers in his fellowship, but they find it by far more comfortable if the pastor, elders and Sunday school teachers serve them, instead of going out to serve others themselves. However, if believers act like this, they will not reach God's goal for their lives.

The parents' problem. The biggest problem parents struggle with is to allow their children to take on adult responsibilities. The children are often very enthusiastic when it comes to trying something new and exciting, but their parents are reluctant to let them do it. Why?

It is too difficult for them to imagine that this child, who was just a baby yesterday, is actually ready and able to handle responsibility. They still want to be that mother hen, who watches over her chicks and at any sign of danger gathers them under her wings. Parents experience fear, knowingly or unknowingly, in letting their children walk toward maturity and independence.

Spiritual parents face the same fear when their "children" come to maturity. For so long they have watched over them, cared for them and protected them; and it is hard to imagine that they could be ready to fight the battle for others. What if they would get hurt or stumble, lose their faith or fail in their outreach work? What if they couldn't heal the sick or cast out the demons? What if a false doctrine or persecution comes their way?

FINDING SOLUTIONS

Whether the maturity problem lies with the believers who refuse to take responsibility or with a church leadership that doesn't allow the believers to "do the work of the ministry," God's kingdom will suffer unless a solution is found.

Teaching and practice. I believe most of the "children's problems" that occur when believers do not want to take responsibility can be solved, or even prevented, by proper teaching and practice. If a new believer is taught from day one what God expects from him when he comes to maturity, he will not be overwhelmed or surprised when the time comes to take responsibility.

If he is permitted to learn step-by-step and to practice what he has learned at the same time, it will be a natural process to make it part of his life. For example, if a new believer is taught how to pray for a sick member of his Sunday school class, later on he will have no problem praying in the same way for those in need in his community.

The best way for a new believer to understand practically what it means to take on responsibility is to grow up in a church in which everyone is about the work of the ministry. When he observes every member performing his or her service according to their maturity level, gifts and calling, he will understand that there is no such thing as a believer without a job in God's kingdom.

Allow them to make mistakes in order to learn. In order for our children to become useful at home and outside the family, they need to have a chance to learn. To solve the "parents' problem," we need to allow them to take on responsibilities that match their maturity levels.

When Sarah was seven years old, she wanted to iron my clothes. I bought her a small play iron at the toy store—one that didn't get hot. But she said, "I don't want this one. I want to do the real thing."

I was afraid because I had burned myself on several occasions, and I never wanted that to happen to her. But then I decided to teach her, and I was surprised at how quickly she learned. Now she irons the school clothes and sometimes my clothes as well. In fact, I count on her help.

Then she wanted to chop vegetables with my big kitchen knife. I told her, "Sarah, I am so scared for you. Look at my finger. See all these scars? They happened with this knife. You first take this small knife and practice cutting the carrots with it. Maybe later I will let you use my big one." I knew it would only be a matter of time before I had to allow her to use my other knife as well.

When my son Daniel asked to ride a big bicycle for the first time, I immediately thought of all the bruises he would have. "Perhaps he should wait," I thought, but his legs were long enough to reach the pedals. I decided to let him have a few bruises and allow him to learn to ride his bike.

When Daniel was younger, he wanted to replace some boards that had broken off of the fence. I warned him to be careful with the hammer and nails and that it would be very painful if he hit his fingers.

In spite of my knowledge that no one has ever learned to handle a hammer without hitting his fingers a few times, I allowed him to go ahead and fix the fence. I knew if I didn't let him try, he could never learn it. He did hit his fingers that day, but he also replaced the boards and fixed the fence. Now I can send him out with a hammer and nails and know without any fear that he is able to do a good job without hurting himself. I know because in the past I permitted him to learn by experience.

For us as parents, it is the hardest thing to choose to let our children make some mistakes while learning to take on responsibility. It is impossible to come to maturity and to gain experience without a few hurts, burns or bruises along the way!

In the same way, pastors, elders and teachers must let their spiritual children go for the purpose God has for them: the work of the ministry (Ephesians 4:12). They must permit them to get a few bruises and make some mistakes as they learn, like David, to run upon a troop and leap over a wall by their God (Psalm 18:29).

Stand back. When Sarah was 11, we visited my parents. Sarah was very eager to do something nice for Grandma, and she asked if she could bake some braided bread for her. Grandma was happy and told her to go ahead.

However, when it came to mixing the ingredients, kneading and braiding the dough, Grandma did all the major parts herself. Every time Sarah was allowed to participate, Grandma would immediately correct what she had just done. Sometimes even in the middle of a procedure Grandma would take the dough out of Sarah's hands and finish it herself. Out of respect, Sarah said nothing, but I was watching her face and knew exactly how she felt.

Very gently, I tried to assure Grandma that Sarah was capable of making the bread by herself, but my approach didn't work. Later, when Sarah and I were alone, she almost cried as she told me, "Mommy, I don't want to bake anything anymore at Grandma's house."

Grandma's intrusion was not because she didn't love Sarah. She loves her very much and would never want to hurt her feelings. But Grandma interfered because she wanted the bread to turn out just perfect. In her mind, it had to look exactly the way she had made it for the past 45 years.

In the church or in team ministry, if we constantly interfere with the tasks that we have given others to do, we will not only discourage people from doing anything at all, but we take away their joy of accomplishment, their enthusiasm and their feeling of ownership. Worst of all, we will cripple individual talents and gifts if everything has to look exactly as if we would have done it ourselves.

Of course, there are things that cannot be compromised, such as doctrines and God's moral laws. But a letter, for example, can be written in more than one way. The same is true for a class taught, an outreach organized and a prayer meeting conducted. God has created each of us so uniquely different, and He intends to work through all of us by using the whole spectrum of personalities, talents and gifts available in His Church.

Just look at the flowers He has made in the field. God displays His love and beauty through them in a thousand different forms and colors. We must not limit Him by trying to fit every believer and his service into one pre-cut mold. This is not only frustrating to attempt to accomplish, but the result is boring. Most of all, it robs the church of many blessings and of many creative avenues to reach out to a lost and dying world.

But how do we stand back and let our "children" take responsibility and learn?

When Sarah wants to bake or cook at our home, I don't stand beside her to watch her every minute. (This *was* necessary when she was small.) I deliberately go and do something else. However, I tell her, "If you need me, call me."

Sometimes she doesn't call me at all. Other times, she will come and ask for my help to determine how much of one ingredient is needed or to check if the food or cake is done. When I wonder how things are progressing, I simply ask her, "How is it going?" instead of looking in the pot to check it out myself.

A few years ago, when Daniel was about 14, our house needed painting on the outside. Daniel wanted to do it during his school vacation. It was a big job, but he felt he could accomplish it.

I talked it over with my husband to get his permission. One of our options was to call some professional painters and have the job done perfectly within two days, without any waste of paint or time. On the other hand, we could allow Daniel to do it, knowing that he would probably need two weeks, possibly more paint, and that the job itself would be a little less than perfect. Of course I had no doubt that his shirt and pants would have paint on them too!

My husband decided that Daniel could paint our house, because he wanted him to have the benefit of learning something new. Because my husband had to travel, I asked one of the brothers in our office to help us get the paint and the brushes and to instruct Daniel how to do the painting.

The brother showed Daniel the correct techniques, and then he left to do his regular job. A few hours later, he returned to see how Daniel was getting along. He advised him how to improve a few things and how to paint more difficult areas such as corners, window frames and door frames before he left again.

During the first few days, he came more often. Later on, he only needed to come once in a while or if Daniel had a question for him. That summer Daniel worked very hard. He not only completed the job, but he did very well.

With my two children, I have found that the most important thing in standing back is to simply be available when needed. I do not want to discourage or intimidate them by watching their every move. And when something goes wrong, I must refrain from criticizing and lecturing and instead find a joyful way to help them fix the problem and encourage them to go on. I am not always good at it, but I am trying to improve my approach.

In a very similar way as a pastor or teacher, you need to learn and practice standing back and allowing your Bible school students, Gospel team members or believers to become able and mature for the work of the ministry. At this point, your role has changed from being a parent to an advisor and counselor. You are still present and available for them if they need you, but only on call.

From time to time, you inspect their work to make sure they are still on track, but you do it in a gentle, supportive way. If you treat them in an encouraging manner, they will feel privileged and eager to show you their progress. They will value your advice and accept your correction.

LET THEM GO

The next step is the final one in our pursuit of bringing God's children to maturity.

God will take your spiritual children from under your care and send them out into this world to build Christ's kingdom. They will encounter battles, persecution, disappointments and victories, but this time (except in a church situation), you will no longer be physically present to solve their problems and fix their mistakes.

This doesn't at all mean that you have abandoned or forgotten them. No—just like a parent, only your role toward your children has changed. Your love has not. You are still an advisor, counselor, pastor or teacher to them, but on a different level.

Paul is the clearest example we have in the New Testament of what it means to change roles from being a parent to an advisor and then to an absent counselor. In the beginning of his church-planting ministry, he was right alongside of the new converts, caring for them and patiently teaching them the ABCs of the Christian faith. When these believers became more mature, he moved on to the next place; but he left co-workers behind to either stay with them or visit them repeatedly. Paul himself visited these congregations again on his second missionary journey. When he saw that these believers had reached the level of maturity to take on responsibility for themselves, he and his co-workers appointed leaders and elders from among each fellowship.

By the time Paul was in prison in Rome, his role of an attentive, nearby parent was completely over. He didn't know how long he had to live before he would lay down his life as a martyr.

However, he was sure that whatever might happen to him, the work he had established would continue. He had trained the believers to do the work of the ministry on their own. He had brought them to a level of maturity at which they were able to depend on the Lord Himself and not on him. He had also discipled and trained men like Timothy and Titus for leadership, men who knew and lived the Gospel message as Paul did.

We don't see Paul in prison retiring and concentrating on his upcoming trial or death. Instead, we see him in a different role: an advisor and counselor to the churches and their leaders. Even if he could not see them for himself, he sent letters or co-workers to them to encourage, correct and strengthen them on his behalf. Most of all, he became an intercessor for all the churches in Asia, bearing their burdens before the Lord:

> For God, whom I serve in my spirit in the preaching of the gospel of His Son, is my witness as to how unceasingly I make mention of you, always in my prayers making request, if perhaps now at last by the will of God I may succeed in coming to you (Romans 1:9-10).

> Apart from such external things, there is the daily pressure upon me of concern for all the churches (2 Corinthians 11:28).

> [I] do not cease giving thanks for you, while making mention of you in my prayers (Ephesians 1:16).

> I thank my God in all my remembrance of you, always offering prayer with joy in my every prayer for you all (Philippians 1:3-4).

> For this reason also, since the day we heard of it, we have not ceased to pray for you and to ask that you may be filled with the knowledge of His will in all spiritual wisdom and understanding (Colossians 1:9).

We give thanks to God always for all of you, making mention of you in our prayers (1 Thessalonians 1:2).

I thank God, whom I serve with a clear conscience the way my forefathers did, as I constantly remember you in my prayers night and day (2 Timothy 1:3).

Perhaps you are a pastor or teacher who has stayed with your congregation for the past 10 years. You feel quite comfortable that your believers depend on you for ministry, teaching, outreach and everything else.

In fact, you would consider it troublesome if suddenly all your believers were doing the work of the ministry and you would have to train, guide and correct them. It frightens you to imagine that your people could have independent ideas and perhaps might want to change some of your traditional church life.

Perhaps you don't feel it necessary to change your approach, because you have no plans to move away and most of these believers will also remain in their village for the rest of their lives. If these are your thoughts, please consider this:

1. *You won't live forever.* What will happen then if these believers cannot stand on their own?

2. *With this thinking, your work will always be limited to what you yourself can handle.* It cannot grow larger.

3. *You have failed to reach God's goal for those He has entrusted to you.* They are supposed to "stand perfect and complete in all the will of God" (Colossians 4:12, KJV), but they are not complete if they are not able to do the work of the ministry without you.

4. *If this transition of parent to advisor in your service to others doesn't take place, you have failed to reach God's goal for yourself as well.*

A pastor's reward is to watch those he has trained and brought to maturity run the race and win the prize.

LIKE A
GRAIN
OF
Wheat

16

SOMEONE HAS TO PAY THE PRICE

*T*wo weeks ago my husband left again for the mission field. I will see him in six weeks.

We were talking together before he left, and he expressed his sadness and concern for leaving me and the children alone so often. I told him, "If I demand everything that is my right to have as a wife and mother, then a hundred years from now, these countries in Asia will still be unreached with the Gospel. Someone has to pay the price."

This is my conviction, and I know it is my husband's as well. If we are not ready ourselves to pay the price, then who else will?

MY RIGHTS

Each of us has expectations and dreams for our lives, such as getting a good education, having a well-paying job, establishing our own business or buying a farm, land or a house. By the time we get married and have a family, we make serious plans about how to raise our children and build our lives. Surely we have the right to live like everyone else in our society and in our church! Why not?

As believers, our expectations are often even higher. We want a godly husband or wife who is responsible, hardworking, caring, loving, sensitive to our needs, an example as a Christian and dedicated to the church and family.

I have my own dreams as well. One of them is just to live completely for my husband and children and spend all my time doing special things for them and for our home. Another dream is to have my husband at home with us and for us to always enjoy a close family relationship and share our lives together.

Many Gospel workers as well have expectations and rights they wish to pursue. Perhaps they want to pastor a well-established church with enough members to ensure a good income. The church should be near a city for convenience's sake, and it should include a nice parsonage with some land around it. After all, the degrees they earned in Bible college or seminary give them the right to have a respected teaching position or a good pastorate. They think, "Let others who don't have those qualifications do the pioneer work."

KNOWING WHAT WE KNOW

Do we not have the right to pursue our dreams like everyone else? Is there anything wrong with this?

No, there is nothing wrong with our rights or with our dreams. But I can speak here for my husband and for myself: I am convinced that we could never really enjoy our dreams and our rights—even if they all became reality—as long as there is a lost world!

How could we have peace and live for ourselves, knowing what we know? We have seen the masses of India and the Subcontinent, desperate, bound in spiritual darkness, without hope, slipping off into hell. How could we demand and pursue a life like everybody else, when millions of people in our generation have never heard the name of Jesus even once?

They Will Only Live if Someone Pays the Price

As the Son of God, Jesus had rights too. But when He saw us, lost without hope and going to hell, He stripped Himself of all He was and of all His rights, so He could come to save us. The Bible says in Philippians 2:7–8: "But [Jesus] emptied Himself, taking the form of a bond-servant, and being made in the likeness of men. And being found in appearance as a man, He humbled Himself by becoming obedient to the point of death, even death on a cross."

Someone had to pay the price for our redemption, and Jesus was the only one qualified to do it. What would our fate have been if He had demanded His rights and not laid them down? We live because Jesus was willing to give up what was rightfully His. The people of our generation will live too, but only if you and I lay down our rights and desires to be like everyone else and pay the price it takes to get the Gospel to them.

My Life Is Not Normal

If I said our family life was normal, it wouldn't be the truth!

As a couple, we have made a deliberate decision that our call to reach the lost world with the Gospel must take priority over our own wishes and desires. Day and night, our thoughts, our talk and our work center around this one goal. Of course, all this has caused our family life to be quite different from those of others. Because of my husband's extensive travel, the children and I are often alone. My responsibilities and work are increased due to his absence. I need to look after the children's school studies, the home, my work in the office and all the details of family life. Of course, I have dear friends to help me, but it is not the same as if my husband could always be at home with us.

Are all my needs as a woman met? *No,* they are not—and *yes,* they are. No—because I often feel lonely. Sometimes I cry and I miss the closeness and fellowship of and talking with my husband. Yes—because I experience the abundant grace, comfort and love of my God who meets my needs. With all of my heart, I can say that I am deeply grateful that my husband has chosen to put God's call first, even if it is not always easy for us. I am in total agreement with him that God's purpose for our lives is more important than our own desires. Even though I am sometimes sad, I wouldn't want to have a different life!

You see, I believe God has called us not to live a normal life, but to be engaged in a war. Wartimes require a different level of commitment and sacrifice from everyone than peacetimes do.

Do we feel deprived? No, we are blessed. Do we regret our decision? No, Jesus is worth it all. Do our children suffer? It is not always easy for them. But God is giving them the same grace that He gives us.

Someone has to pay the price for a lost world to know Jesus. Why should it not be our generation that will complete the task of "making disciples of all nations"?

17

LOVE MATCHES
THE PRICE

As a pastor, evangelist or Bible woman, you will meet many different people on your outreach. Sometimes you will find it hard to love them, especially when they are so hostile and disinterested in your message.

You will have believers in your fellowship who let you do all the work alone and don't ever seem to mature to the point of being willing to help carry the load. Then there will be others who make you wonder if your sacrifices of time, energy and prayers are doing any good at all and if they are really worth the effort. You will feel stretched in every way, and you will struggle to love these people.

Let me share something with you that has helped me greatly in finding love for those to whom the Lord sent me.

I was sitting on a chair on the platform during one of my ladies' meetings, enjoying the singing and worship and waiting for my time to speak. As I looked over the audience, an old village woman who was sitting in the front row on a straw mat caught my attention. Her face was wrinkled and dark from the sun. There were not many teeth left in her mouth, and it was difficult to estimate her age. The clothes she wore were very simple and inexpensive. I wondered if she had enough education to be able to read the Bible.

While I was looking at her, the Lord began to speak to my heart. "This village woman," He said, "is very precious to Me. I love her, and she is worth so much to Me that I broke you for her, so that you will be able to minister to her."

These words were totally unexpected, and they really hit me hard. I tried to grasp their meaning. Could it be that all I had encountered during my Christian walk was for her? The many struggles, the trials, the disappointments, the tears, the sacrifices and the continuous breaking of myself were actually God's preparation for me to be able to minister to this woman's needs? What a price God was paying for her!

I was amazed to think how much Jesus must love her, that He was willing to break me on her behalf. All of a sudden I didn't see an old village woman any more. I looked at a person who was extremely valuable in the sight of Jesus, and I had the privilege of being a servant to her.

I never forgot this experience. God has used this old lady to give me a completely new perspective on the value God placed on the souls He had ordained to cross the path of my life. To me, I would never have considered some of them as "targets" or goals to invest my time and effort into their lives. But I learned that God's thoughts on their value to Him and His kingdom are obviously different from mine.

I discovered that my love grew instantly for this old lady, and for others as well, when I looked at them and told myself: "She (or he) is worth it in the eyes of God for me to be broken."

It is not only you whom God breaks for others, but others have been broken for you, so that they could minister to your needs and help you grow. There is the pastor who led you to the Lord, your Sunday school teacher who helped you understand the Bible, the old believer who prayed so faithfully for you every time you were in trouble, the grandmother who took you in and treated you like a son when you were thrown out of your home because of your faith. Just think, God broke them and prepared their lives in a special way so that they could truly love you and help you.

Then there is Jesus, of whom Isaiah 53:5 says: "But He was pierced through for our transgressions, He was crushed for our iniquities."

You are so precious in the eyes of God the Father that He was willing to break Jesus on your behalf. The amazing love Jesus has for you matches the high price He paid for your redemption.

As a servant of God, you will find your love for others grow dramatically when you understand the value that God has placed on souls and what it actually cost God to break Jesus, His only Son, and you, His beloved child, for their sake.

What is the secret of a mother's love for her baby and her willingness to die for it if necessary? Is it not the price she paid, the suffering she went through and the facing of death as she gave birth?

The love you will have for others will be in direct proportion to the price you pay for them. They will live because of your dying.

18

CONSIDERED WORTHY

*M*ost Sunday mornings the children and I get ready to go to our church—alone without my husband. He is either on some mission field, or he is preaching somewhere out of town. Only a few times a year is he able to come with us.

Every Sunday I see others arriving at church as families and later going home to spend the afternoon together. Because my children attend their own classes or sit with their age groups, most of the people at church see me by myself.

On one particular Sunday, one of the ladies asked me: "Is your husband gone to India again? When will he be back?"

"In five weeks," I replied.

She looked at me sadly and asked, "Isn't that hard for you?"

"Yes, it is sometimes," I answered, "but because of the ministry, this is what we have decided for our lives."

A few minutes later, another woman greeted me. Knowing my husband was on a mission trip, she asked, "Are you all right? You are often so quiet."

When the service started and everyone began singing, I still was thinking about the two conversations I just had. Sometimes people seem to feel sorry for me and other times they wonder how I can live like this. There are times when I feel sorry for myself as well!

But this Sunday, the Lord asked me to look at my life in a different light. All of a sudden, I remembered the story in Acts 5:17–42 where Peter and John were arrested, beaten and threatened by the Council in Jerusalem for preaching the name of Jesus. Verse 41 says, "So they went on their way from the presence of the Council, rejoicing that they had been considered worthy to suffer shame for His name."

Right then the Lord told me in my heart, "You are considered worthy to be alone for My sake."

I was really surprised by this. My sacrifices seemed so small to me, especially in the light of such a Bible verse that talks about real persecution, martyrdom and self-denial.

The more I thought about this "being considered worthy" by God Himself, my going to church alone and the weeks or months spent without my husband looked like a privilege I received from heaven, rather than a hardship that I had to accept and endure as part of the ministry. Some years ago I was really touched by the statement Paul wrote to the Philippian Christians: "For to you it has been granted for Christ's sake, not only to believe in Him, but also to suffer for His sake" (Philippians 1:29).

I recognized that it was indeed a special grace, actually a grant, that was given to these believers to suffer for Christ's sake. It was not a privilege they had earned but a gift bestowed on them.

In the eyes of heaven, there seems to be no higher honor for a Christian than to be allowed to suffer for Jesus. Yet in the middle of persecution and hardship, it is often very difficult for us to have this heavenly perspective.

However, I never knew what criterion God uses when He gives this grant of "not only to believe in Him, but also to suffer for His sake." But after looking at Acts 5:41, the criterion became very clear to me: ". . . they had been considered worthy to suffer shame for His name." According to this verse, the Lord passes out the grant of suffering because He has considered someone worthy for the highest honor heaven has to offer!

What giants of Christians are these people who have managed to qualify for this heavenly honor roll? And what about the others who didn't make it?

After reading and comparing a number of other Scriptures in the New Testament, I believe that simply because we are children of the King of kings, God actually considers *all* of us worthy to suffer for Christ's sake. How else would you interpret these words of Jesus and some of the writers of the New Testament:

> And *you* will be hated by all on account of My name (Matthew 10:22).

> If *any one* wishes to come after Me, let him deny himself, and take up his cross, and follow Me. For *whoever* wishes to save his life shall lose it; but whoever loses his life for My sake shall find it (Matthew 16:24–25).

> Unless a grain of wheat falls into the earth and dies, it remains by itself alone; but if it dies, it bears much fruit. He who loves his life loses it; and he who hates his life in this world shall keep it to life eternal. If any one serves Me, let him follow Me; and where I am, there shall My servant also be; if *any one* serves Me, the Father will honor him (John 12:24–26).

> Therefore Jesus also, that He might sanctify the people through His own blood, suffered outside the gate. Hence, *let us* go out to Him outside the camp, bearing His reproach (Hebrews 13:12–13).

> And indeed, all who desire to live godly in Christ Jesus will be persecuted (2 Timothy 3:12).

All these verses reveal two things to us. First, there is a natural hatred or rejection that we will face from the world and its systems because we are Christians and citizens of another world. Second, there is an added suffering that is the result of our own choice when we decide to deny ourselves, follow after Him, take up our cross, serve Him, die to ourselves in order to bear fruit and go out of the camp to bear His reproach.

Why, then, if all of us are considered worthy to suffer for Christ's sake, do most believers reject even the thought of it? I believe there are two main reasons for this attitude:

We don't consider suffering shame as an honor or something we value to have. The prospect of suffering in any form is not appealing to our flesh at all. We try to avoid it at all costs. Every time we are faced with discomfort or even asked for a small sacrifice on behalf of the Gospel, we immediately retreat, try to find a way out or around, or we seek to pray it away or cast it out. In other words, when God offers us the honor of suffering for Christ's sake or denying ourselves in order to follow Him, we don't accept it.

We are afraid of the extent to which it will take us. We reason: "If God asks me today to give up my job or my money for the Gospel, what will He ask from me tomorrow?"

It is largely a matter of how deep I want to go with my commitment to follow Christ and how far I allow myself to trust Him with the life I hold so dear. Nowhere in the Bible do we read that the Lord needs all of us to die as martyrs, leave our countries or sit for years in a prison cell.

According to His wisdom, God's plan is different for each of us, and so is the measure of suffering and self-denial required to complete the task. What He needs are servants who have no reservations on their lives, servants who are willing to accept the honor to gladly lay down anything, whether big or small, the Lord may need to build His kingdom.

As sure as the Lord called you to serve Him, there will come times when you are called upon to accept persecution, suffering and sacrifice for the sake of the Gospel and the millions of people lost and dying without Christ.

Train yourself not to look at these things as burdens you have to somehow endure by gritting your teeth and facing them with sheer boldness. If you approach it that way, you will eventually end up feeling sorry for yourself. You will shed tears of self-pity, and you will look with envy at others who seem to have it so much better and definitely easier.

When you struggle within yourself to accept suffering and self-denial, stop and look full into the face of the Son of God and say to yourself with amazement:

> I am considered worthy in the sight of God to bear this loneliness for Jesus' sake.

> I am considered worthy to walk this 20 kilometers to this tribal village.

> I am considered worthy to climb this mountain carrying this box of literature on my shoulders.

> I am considered worthy to let my husband (my son, my daughter) go to the mission field.

> I am considered worthy to give up the time I wanted to have for myself in order to extend His kingdom.

One more thing: If you are a Gospel worker and you are married, share this concept of being "considered worthy" with your wife and, if possible, with your children. They are the ones who often have to bear so much as they walk alongside you. But *please* don't use this to apply pressure on them or keep them from complaining. Share it only as encouragement and to strengthen them.

There is great joy that comes with understanding the honor

of suffering for Jesus. We can clearly see this in the lives of Peter and John as well as in those of Paul and Silas:

> So they [Peter and John] went on their way from the presence of the Council, rejoicing that they had been considered worthy to suffer shame for His name (Acts 5:41).

> And when they had inflicted many blows upon them, they . . . threw them into the inner prison, and fastened their feet in the stocks. But about midnight Paul and Silas were praying and singing hymns of praise to God (Acts 16:23-25).

I too experienced this joy when I understood God's perspective on being "considered worthy" to give up something for Jesus' sake.

That Sunday in church, my friend was sitting beside me with her husband and their little daughter. She works so hard and so faithfully in our ministry, editing books, writing letters, making phone calls and all this besides caring for her home and family. She is doing it by giving up a lot of her own plans and her time. I looked at her and wondered if she realized that God considered her worthy to give up these things for Christ's sake. I decided to share this with her the next time she felt overwhelmed with God's plans and her own expectations of being a wife and mother.

As we serve the Lord, we must never lose the amazement that God has "considered us worthy" to lay down something we wanted for ourselves—for Jesus' sake.

UNTIL WE
SEE HIS
Face

19

GOD TOOK HIM
FROM THE SHEEP

Whenever the Lord Jesus talked about us as His followers, He seemed to have much higher expectations of the influence and outcome of our lives than we would ever consider.

Let us look at John 7:38. Leaving no room for doubt, Jesus declared this: "He who believes in Me, as the Scripture said, 'From his innermost being shall flow rivers of living water.'"

I believe the Lord expects each of us to come to a point in our Christian walk at which these rivers of living water will indeed flow out of our lives into this world. Anything less than rivers is falling short of God's goal and our realistic potential as believers.

When I consider my own life in the light of this Bible verse, I must honestly say that I cannot see any rivers. Sometimes I have noticed drops of living water, occasionally a small trickle and perhaps a little creek. But according to Jesus' statement, I know for sure that I have not yet become all that God wants me to be.

In the Bible we read about a number of people from whose lives those rivers of living water were truly flowing. One of them was David. God chose and anointed David while he was very young. His first deed was to kill Goliath the Philistine and bring a great victory to Israel. From that time onward, his life was the cause of continuous blessing for Israel as well as victory over their enemies.

Before David became king, there was much chaos in the land. Saul had not at all been a man and king after God's heart, but David was. Not only did he provide excellent political leadership, but throughout his life, David also actively worked to lead his people in the ways of the Lord.

Spiritually, David was a very sensitive, man and he sought God with all his heart. As a leader, he allowed God to work His purpose through his life; as a prophet, he permitted God to use him as His mouthpiece. When we read the psalms David wrote, we can easily see the deep walk this man had with God. His whole country and all those in his kingdom were blessed because of it.

First Chronicles 18:14 testifies to this: "So David reigned over all Israel; and he administered justice and righteousness for all his people." Because of David's faithfulness, humility and obedience to God, not only were all of Israel's enemies subdued, but rivers of living water were truly flowing from his life to his people.

At the height of his glory, David had a special desire in his heart. We read about this in 1 Chronicles 17. He shared it with Nathan the prophet. In essence, he said, "I have done so many things and a lot of it was for myself, but now I want to build a house for the Lord." God was very pleased with David's desire, and He sent a reply to David through the prophet Nathan. God told him, "It is a wonderful thing that you want to build My house, but I don't want you to do it. Your son after you shall do it. David, I am very pleased with you, and I have decided to bless your home and to establish your throne and kingdom forever."

When David saw God's grace and loving-kindness toward him, he went and sat before the Lord, simply amazed and awed by the love and compassion of the God of Israel for him, a man who used to be a nobody.

When Nathan brought God's message to David, God instructed him exactly how he was to address David: "Thus says the LORD of hosts, 'I took you from the pasture, from following the sheep, that you should be leader over My people Israel' " (1 Chronicles 17:7).

This was at a time in David's life when rivers of living water were flowing from David to his people, and God was very much aware of it. Did God have a reason to tell David, "I took you from the sheep," before He said anything further?

Yes. I believe God had a very specific concern in mind to address David the way He did. There was a reason that He did not tell him first: "David, you are a great man, an excellent leader, a famous king . . ." You see, God knows that when we have success in our lives and ministries and when rivers of living water flow from us, we are in great danger of thinking highly of ourselves.

A very vivid example of this is King Nebuchadnezzar. We read in Daniel 4:29–30 how he looked at the city of Babylon and then said to himself: "Is this not Babylon the great, which I myself have built as a royal residence by the might of my power and for the glory of my majesty?" Subsequent verses describe the immediate judgment upon this king because of the pride in his heart. For seven years he was insane, forsaken by all, living like an animal—until he humbled himself.

Many leaders and Christian workers have suffered their greatest defeats immediately following the time when God used them the most. They forgot where they were when God first took them and began to use them. They attributed their achievements to their own abilities instead of God's mercy.

God deliberately reminded David of the sheep because He wanted to warn and protect him from falling in the trap of seeing himself as a great man instead of someone who depended totally on God's grace. When God said, "I took you from the pasture," He meant this: "David, never forget that when I picked you up, you were nothing. All you knew then, all you did, was herd sheep. Everything you are now, the distance you have come, and all your success are by My grace alone. You have come through many trials and suffering to the position you are in now. It was all My plan and My love for you. If I took My hand off you today, you would be right back with the sheep. As rivers of living water flow now from your life, be very careful that you give the glory to Me, otherwise you might fall."

God knew the heart of His servant, but He also could see further ahead in David's life. He saw the temptations that would come his way, and He wanted to warn him to stay humble. He wanted David to be prepared to counter Satan's attacks with the right spiritual weapons and attitude of heart.

David responded to God's message with true humility. His prayer in 1 Chronicles 17:16–27 acknowledged God's grace that brought him from the sheep to the throne. Many of David's psalms express this same conviction—that he was nothing and his God had become everything to him. And in 2 Samuel 22:2–3, David says, "The LORD is my rock and my fortress and my deliverer; my God, my rock, in whom I take refuge; my shield and the horn of my salvation, my stronghold and my refuge."

GOD LOOKS FOR SHEPHERDS

The people of Israel were surrounded by heathen nations whose kings and leaders ruled their people by force, oppression and position. This was normal practice in those days, and life in general was very cheap.

But it was not to be this way at all in Israel. God Himself

had laid down different principles than those of the nations on their borders. The people of Israel were His own possession and extremely precious in His sight. Therefore, when He selected leaders, judges, prophets and kings for them, He always looked for someone with a shepherd's heart.

When God selected Moses to lead His people out of slavery, Moses' upbringing and experience in the palace of Pharaoh didn't qualify him for the job. Undoubtedly, Moses had received the best training possible, which an Egyptian ruler would need to sit on the throne, but he knew nothing about sheep and being a shepherd. God had to make him a shepherd, with 40 years of training and experience, before He could make Moses a leader of Israel.

When God told Moses in Numbers 27:12–13 that he was to die soon, Moses had but one single concern:

> May the LORD, the God of the spirits of all flesh, appoint a man over the congregation, who will go out and come in before them, and who will lead them out and bring them in, that the congregation of the LORD may not be like sheep which have no shepherd (Numbers 27:16–17).

Until that day, Moses did not know who would lead Israel after his death. Contrary to the customs of the time, he did not groom or automatically appoint one of his sons or close relatives for this position. He knew it had to be God's choice, because He alone was able to discern the heart of a man. All Moses did was ask God to give Israel a man with a shepherd's heart who would be concerned for their welfare just as he had been.

In the following verse we read that God chose Joshua, not because he was experienced in battle or because he had served under Moses, but because God's Spirit was in him (Numbers 27:18). This Spirit would enable Joshua to know God's heart and therefore shepherd His people the way God wanted it done.

Joshua definitely had the advantage of always remembering Moses' example as a shepherd and could practice what he had observed when he served under Moses. However, God gave Joshua, and every leader who would come after him, very specific instructions for becoming a qualified and successful shepherd and for knowing exactly what to do in leadership:

> Only be strong and very courageous; be careful to do according to all the law which Moses My servant commanded you; do not turn from it to the right or to the left, so that you may have success wherever you go. This book of the law shall not depart from your mouth, but you shall meditate on it day and night, so that you may be careful to do according to all that is written in it; for then you will make your way prosperous, and then you will have success (Joshua 1:7-8).

This command of God is as relevant today as it was then. As servants of God, as leaders and shepherds, we must deliberately and continuously expose our minds and hearts to the Word of God, so that no human wisdom is able to rule us. Only then will we be able to lead God's people in God's way.

In the Old Testament, everyone the Lord called into leadership was to be in total obedience to Him and to take His orders. God never gave them the liberty to do their own thing, copy other nations or have absolute power. On the contrary, God assigned "watchdogs," or prophets, alongside each king or leader. Even the most rebellious ones like Ahab had prophets who, at the risk of their lives, told them the will of God. These prophets were meant to be an added blessing, protection and strength for the leader. They were given by God to help carry the burdens and assist the leaders in knowing the will of God for their nation.

God never gave any of the leaders He called the permission to rule, only to lead and to shepherd. This becomes very clear when we read Psalm 23. In this psalm, God reveals His own heart toward His people: a shepherd's heart. This song describes how God our Father goes about shepherding His flock: He goes before them, never leaving them alone; He cares for them and leads them to places where they are able to find food, water and rest; He watches out for their welfare, protects them and comforts them; and going ahead of them, He faces the dangers of the valley of the shadow of death first and leads them through without deserting or confusing them.

Isaiah 40:11, Psalm 147:3 and many other Scriptures throughout the Bible also describe how the Lord our Shepherd cares for His sheep. He binds up their wounds and carries those who cannot walk themselves. The sheep are satisfied and happy, able to trust their Shepherd completely, knowing that He always seeks the best for them.

These Scriptures do not occur by accident in the Bible. God has placed them there for all those whom He calls into leadership. They are a perfect picture and instruction of what leadership means and what God expects from His servants.

In the New Testament we find these same principles for leading a church. Leading and shepherding are totally different from ruling. When Jesus came, He did not proclaim Himself as ruler, but as a shepherd: "I am the good shepherd; the good shepherd lays down His life for the sheep" (John 10:11).

In Luke 15:4-6, Jesus describes how He, the Shepherd, goes after one lost sheep until He finds it, carrying it home on His shoulders, rejoicing. That is exactly what God had in mind when He called David, or anyone else, to lead His people.

Jesus instructed His disciples about leadership in this way: "The greatest among you shall be your servant" (Matthew 23:11). What does this mean? The one whose life produces much fruit for the kingdom of God and from whom rivers of living water flow to others must lead by becoming a servant of all.

Peter had denied the Lord three times. When Jesus restored him, He specifically commissioned Peter: "Tend My lambs . . . shepherd My sheep . . . tend My sheep" (John 21:15–17).

Jesus told Peter that he must care for God's people as a shepherd would. Peter never forgot this. Later in his life, when he trained others for leadership, he wrote them these instructions:

> Therefore, I exhort the elders among you, as your fellow-elder and witness of the sufferings of Christ, and a partaker also of the glory that is to be revealed, shepherd the flock of God among you, not under compulsion, but voluntarily, according to the will of God; and not for sordid gain, but with eagerness; nor yet as lording it over those allotted to your charge, but proving to be examples to the flock. And when the Chief Shepherd appears, you will receive the unfading crown of glory (1 Peter 5:1–4).

Paul also understood that to lead God's people meant laying down his life for them as a shepherd would. He wrote, "I will most gladly spend and be expended for your souls" (2 Corinthians 12:15).

A servant and shepherd will seek to build up others. He considers their welfare above his own. A ruler, however, will seek to please himself at the expense of others.

When Israel wanted a king to rule over them, just like all the other nations, Samuel warned them about all that this king would demand—the best of their land, their flocks, their sons and daughters for his service—and that he would do whatever pleased him with their lives (1 Samuel 8:10–18).

WHEN DAVID FORGOT THE SHEEP

Every time one of God's appointed leaders forgets that he was taken from following the sheep, he will start ruling instead of serving. He, as well as his people, will be in great danger.

God had deliberately reminded David one more time in 1 Chronicles 17 of his sheep and his low beginning, so David could focus on staying humble when temptation approached him. However, a few chapters later, we already see that David had completely forgotten God's warning. We read this story in 1 Chronicles 21:1–7 and 14:

> Then Satan stood up against Israel and moved David to number Israel. So David said to Joab and to the princes of the people, "Go, number Israel from Beersheba even to Dan, and bring me word that I may know their number."
>
> And Joab said, "May the LORD add to His people a hundred times as many as they are! But, my lord the king, are they not all my lord's servants? Why does my lord seek this thing? Why should he be a cause of guilt to Israel?"
>
> Nevertheless, the king's word prevailed against Joab. Therefore, Joab departed and went throughout all Israel, and came to Jerusalem. And Joab gave the number of the census of all the people to David. And all Israel were 1,100,000 men who drew the sword; and Judah was 470,000 men who drew the sword. But he did not number Levi and Benjamin among them, for the king's command was abhorrent to Joab.
>
> And God was displeased with this thing, so He struck Israel. So the LORD sent a pestilence on Israel; 70,000 men of Israel fell.

When David gave Joab the command to number the fighting force of Israel, he was no longer acting as a shepherd who would protect the sheep. It was absolutely against God's command for anyone to number the people of Israel. God wanted David as well as the people to trust in Him when they had to face their enemies in battle and not to rely on numbers. David's order was something that both he and Joab knew was directly opposed to the will of God.

Joab, David's commander-in-chief, summoned the courage to confront David and tell him that he was about to bring God's wrath down on all of them (v. 3). But verse 4 tells us that the king's word prevailed. In other words, David told Joab: "You'd better do what I told you to do. Don't question my decision—I am the king here."

David was speaking here as a ruler who wanted to please himself. He was no longer acting and speaking as a servant and shepherd who was willing to lay down his life for his sheep.

When we read further in this chapter, we learn the result of David's actions. God was very displeased, and He sent a pestilence in the land. Seventy thousand men of Israel died from it.

David acknowledged that he had sinned greatly. He repented, and God forgave him. But imagine: The man from whom rivers of living water were flowing had become the single reason for 70,000 families to dig graves to bury loved ones! God had warned him to remember that He took him from following the sheep, but he forgot.

In 2 Samuel 11, another event took place when David again forgot that he was supposed to be a shepherd.

David's army was at war, but he had stayed home instead. In the evening when he was on the roof of his house, he saw a beautiful woman taking her bath. He inquired about her and found out she was Bathsheba, the wife of Uriah, one of his warriors. He sent for her and committed adultery with her. When she got pregnant, he tried to cover up his sin by calling her husband back home from the front lines, so later on he would think the child was his own. However, when this plan didn't work, David arranged Uriah's death.

David's actions in this account were not the result of falling into temptation by accident. Instead, each act was premeditated and well-planned. Satan's attack on this man of God must have been very severe for David to heap one terrible sin on top of another.

If he looked around at other nations, however, he could justify his actions. He was acting like any other king. At that time, kings had the power of life and death in their hands. It was nothing for them to execute someone who stood in their way.

But God's principles for being a leader of His people were so different. He wanted them to lay down their lives for the people, not to take advantage of them.

Every time David ruled his people rather than leading and shepherding them, he destroyed the lives of others. Even though he repented with all his heart, the dead did not rise again, and those who were hurt by his actions had to live with their wounds.

David himself had to bear the consequences of his sins in his own family. The child that was born to Bathsheba died. Tamar, his daughter, was raped by her half-brother, Amnon. Absalom, Tamar's brother, killed Amnon out of revenge. Later, Absalom tried to take the kingdom from David and was killed in the process.

David also had to face the humiliation of his sins being made public before his people and the nations around him. Not only that, his acts were recorded in the Chronicles of the Kings, to be read by all the generations to come.

We must remember that these things took place during the time of David's life when rivers of living water were flowing from him.

God has also taken each one of us from following the sheep. We have received a call to build His kingdom, but we must never forget where we came from! Without God's call, we would still follow idols or live just for ourselves like all our relatives. We would plant rice fields, work in a shop or office and earn a living. But now we are given the privilege of being servants of the living God.

When these rivers of living water start flowing from our lives and when we experience success and blessing like David did, we must be very careful not to forget the sheep. As servants of God, if we ever forget that we were nothing when God found us, we are in great danger of ruling instead of serving. All we are today is because of His grace alone.

We can count on it—every time we rule, we will destroy others. But every time we serve and lay down our lives, we will build up others, and more living water will start flowing out of our lives to a lost and dying world.

20

FOCUS ON
THE OUTCOME

A few years ago, I was sitting in our church during the worship service. The choir sang some beautiful songs, and then the pastor began to preach. But that Sunday morning, I was not listening to any of it.

My mind was occupied with something else. I was thinking about the letters we had recently received from several mission fields. Some of the reports were heartbreaking, and I realized once again how much suffering is involved on the part of the missionaries to take the Gospel to the rest of India and Asia. The more I thought about all this, the more I became sad in my heart. I said to myself and to the Lord, "The cost is too high."

How much prayer, fasting and money are needed to make any impact for the Gospel on a pioneer field?

The brothers and sisters in our home office have to carry so many burdens and work so hard for endless hours.

Then there are those who travel constantly to the mission fields and are gone from their families for long periods of time. When they come home, they have lost 20 pounds due to lack of sleep and proper food and the rough ways they must travel.

Our leaders have to carry so many responsibilities and often have to make difficult decisions. Some of them are young and are afraid to make mistakes because it will affect many other people as well. It is a lonely life to be a leader. Whenever something goes wrong, they are the ones who face criticism and accusations.

Then there are our brothers and sisters working on the mission fields in India and the rest of Asia, who have to pay such a high price of suffering and persecution before even one church is established. Every year we receive reports about some who have died as martyrs or were severely persecuted for the sake of the Gospel. Consider these examples:

> One missionary in Orissa was beaten and tied up over a fire made from his Bibles and Gospel literature, until 60 percent of his skin was burned.

> In Sri Lanka, a brother was shot to death while preaching before his congregation at the altar.

> In Rajasthan, a brother was forced by his relatives, who hated his faith in Jesus, to drink acid until he was severely burned internally.

> While on the way home from an outreach, a missionary in Tamil Nadu was murdered and then sawed into four pieces.

> A brother in Karnataka state was preaching in his church when men with iron bars walked in and beat him. His wrist and legs were broken. The attackers threatened his wife and the congregation as well. When his little son saw his father beaten, he cried out, "Don't kill my Daddy!" The men turned on this little seven-year-old boy and beat him with iron bars until his back was broken.

Perhaps you can understand why I felt sad on that Sunday morning and why I wondered how we could bear such a high cost to win these nations. I thought as well about the wives and children of these missionaries, who daily have to live with the reality that their husband or father might never come back. These families suffer more than most of us can imagine.

I also thought about my husband. For more than half of the year, he is gone to other countries. We do not see him much. When he comes home, he is so tired and exhausted, and I wonder how long he can keep it up.

But on that Sunday in my church, when I said, "Lord, the cost is too high," He helped me see something in the Bible that I had not seen before.

When you read this book, you might be just finishing Bible school and getting ready to enter your ministry. Maybe you have been challenged by the testimonies and the dedication of pioneer missionaries, who indeed paid the high price I described earlier. You have heard God's call on your life, and you have dedicated yourself to serve the Lord in one of these places where the Gospel has never before been preached.

I don't know how you feel. But behind your smile and your "Praise the Lord," you might feel afraid, wondering whether you can face such a cost and if you are strong enough to bear such mental pressure and physical hardship. Of course, you are willing to go and serve the Lord, and you believe in the Holy Spirit; but you are afraid to face the cost.

I believe we need to learn to bear the cost, just as Jesus bore it when He was on earth. Our salvation cost Jesus His whole life. We need to see how Jesus faced the price tag of our salvation.

JESUS KNEW THE TOTAL COST
Before Jesus ever came to this earth and when He entered His ministry at age 30, He was not at all ignorant of what it

would cost Him to purchase our salvation. He knew very well that persecution, the cross and ultimately death were waiting for Him. He thought, talked and prayed about it. Jesus lived with the knowledge of the total cost it would take to redeem this world.

We are different. We don't know what tomorrow will bring. Many times we worry about things in our lives that never will happen at all. We are afraid of getting sick, losing a loved one or possibly getting beaten up in North India. When the time comes, we realize that none of these things happened after all, and we worried for nothing.

God is merciful to allow us to deal only with our daily hardships. He knows that we would get too frightened and perhaps lose courage altogether to follow His call if we knew our tomorrows, including the cost to fulfill our ministry.

But with Jesus it was different. He didn't just know a small portion of His tomorrow. No—He knew the full range of the price that it would take to redeem us.

How did Jesus know this? For one thing, every time He took a scroll of the Old Testament and began to read the prophets— Isaiah, Jeremiah and on down the list—He was reading about His own life. As He was growing up, He would hear the teachers in the synagogue explaining the Scriptures, and He would realize, "They are talking about Me."

Every detail of His life was written in the prophets. He could see and read what would happen to Him in the years to come. He knew He would be betrayed by a friend, spit upon, despised and rejected by the whole nation of Israel. They would nail Him to a cross. God would lay all sickness and the sin of the whole world upon Him. He would have to die on that cross, alone without His Father. God would turn away from Him and leave Him in the hand of Satan. But then, after three days, He would rise again.

How do you think this knowledge about His life affected Jesus when He was a teenager and later a young man there in His hometown? I believe He must have been very serious and greatly motivated to study the Scriptures and to go to the synagogue to learn everything He possibly could from the rabbis.

As He entered His ministry, Jesus knew every detail of the cost for Him to redeem us because of His knowledge of the Word of God. He was not only aware of what was waiting for Him, but He also knew He needed to fulfill every little thing written about Him, without leaving out even one of them.

Not only could Jesus read about His life, but He was also able to see beforehand how the Romans scourged and crucified a criminal. The Romans were the occupying force in Palestine, and any kind of death sentence had to be carried out according to their laws and by their soldiers. It was a very common form of execution to nail the prisoners to a cross and leave them hanging there until death finally took place.

Jesus surely must have seen many times how they drove the nails through the wrists and feet of such a condemned man, how they erected the cross and the many hours of suffering it would take to die like this. Jesus was not ignorant of what He was approaching in His ministry. Every time He passed by a Roman execution, He had to tell Himself, "This is waiting for Me."

And then He knew one more thing, the most horrible thing of all: There at the cross, He would fall into the hands of Satan and his demons, while God would turn His face away from Him. Jesus knew Satan very well from eternity past. He witnessed Satan's revolt in the heavenlies, and He saw him and his followers cast out of heaven. Jesus knew exactly how wicked and how powerful Satan was and the wrath of which he was capable. Jesus knew very well what it meant to fall into the hands of Satan and his demon forces and what they would do to Him. Such a horrible, unthinkable darkness would come over His soul as

He would bear the punishment of every sin on earth—past, present and future. For Jesus, who never sinned Himself and who was the Light of the World, it must have been the most terrifying thought that He would have to pay that ultimate price.

Jesus had all these things daily before His eyes. These events moved closer and closer as His ministry expanded. However, when we read the Scripture, we find that Jesus walked steadfastly toward the cross, without detour, without changing His mind, without hesitation.

He walked to that cross fully aware of what was about to happen and what He would have to pay to purchase our salvation. As the months and years went by, He could say to Himself, "Three more years until the cross . . . now it is two years . . . now five months . . . now it is two weeks."

In Luke 9:51 we read that when the time had come for Him to die, He set His face resolutely toward Jerusalem. He never looked back.

How could Jesus live as He did and bear the pressure? He was not a superman; neither did He retain some supernatural powers to help Him over the difficulties. The Bible tells us very clearly in Philippians 2:7-8 that he emptied Himself of everything that had distinguished Him from us as human beings.

He indeed felt our pain and suffering, He encountered the same fears as we do, He faced the same temptations and human struggles and He was subject to the same mental pressure as we are (see Hebrews 2:18, 4:15).

Yes, He was the Son of God; but through salvation, we also are sons and daughters of God. Jesus was called and anointed by God to His ministry, but so are we. He was filled with the same Holy Spirit that fills us. God did not have a different, more powerful Holy Spirit for Jesus and another lesser one for us! Jesus had no secret power that is not available to us also!

When He faced battles, He had to use exactly the same

weapons of warfare that we are given. He had to pray before making decisions, to get answers to His petitions and for strength. Jesus had to use faith to perform miracles, heal the sick and raise the dead. To fight off temptations, He had to use the Sword of the Spirit: the Word of God. He had to depend on the power of the Holy Spirit for anything He needed to do in His ministry.

Jesus totally identified with us. Yet He was able to face the cost of our redemption without trembling in His heart, wondering if He could do it—and without walking away.

Jesus Walked in the Shadow of the Price

Jesus walked daily in the shadow of the cross and the price He knew it would take to redeem this world. How could Jesus sleep at night knowing all that would happen to Him? How was He able to have peace with this horror hanging over His head? How did He manage to not become discouraged, to not complain and to not give up or change His mind?

How could He prevent Himself from calling a legion of angels from heaven to fight for Him? How was He able to maintain His willingness to pay such a high price until the very end?

How was Jesus able to live with this daily mental pressure without crumbling under it? We see the real extent of this pressure in Gethsemane, when His human fear, the mental pressure and a spiritual confrontation between heaven and hell all closed in on Him.

Jesus' approach to facing the cost in the midst of all this was no different from how we as believers would do it: He was obedient to His Father in all things, and He maintained an unbroken relationship with Him through constant prayer and fellowship. Jesus used Scripture, the power of the Holy Spirit and all His spiritual weapons to fight His warfare. Besides all this, He maintained His love for His Father and for us throughout His life.

We usually stop here with our efforts, but Jesus didn't.

JESUS FOCUSED ON THE OUTCOME

The Bible tells us that Jesus did one more thing in order to bear the cost for our redemption: *He deliberately focused on the outcome and not on the cost.* We read this in Hebrews 12:1-2: "Let us run with endurance the race that is set before us, fixing our eyes on Jesus, the author and perfecter of faith, *who for the joy set before Him endured the cross,* despising the shame, and has sat down at the right hand of the throne of God."

Jesus purposely did not put the cost before His eyes, but rather the joy He would have *after* He had completed His work. He did not concentrate on the pain, suffering and shame He would have to bear, but He used all His energies to concentrate His mind and His heart on the joy after the cross.

He thought about the joy it would be to have pleased the Father and fulfilled the Scriptures, the joy to think about you and me and to know He made it possible for us to have salvation, the joy to be able to go back to heaven. Most of all, Jesus thought and concentrated on the joy of that moment He had longed for from eternity past, when He finally could cry out: "It is finished."

Focusing on the joy that would follow all the suffering made it possible for Jesus to walk daily under the shadow of the cross, without breaking under the pressure. Jesus had to keep His concentration on the joy *after* the cross throughout His life and ministry. He knew that if He allowed His mind to slip and started focusing on the cost, He might not be able to make it until the end.

The devil, of course, tried to make Jesus lose His focus by using Peter. Matthew 16:21-23 tells us about this encounter. Jesus was sharing with His disciples that very soon He would have to go to Jerusalem, suffer many things, be killed and then rise again.

Peter took Him aside and rebuked Him, saying, "God forbid it, Lord! This shall never happen to You" (v. 22). Jesus immediately recognized Satan's attack, and He said to Peter, "Get behind Me, Satan! You are a stumbling block to Me; for you are not setting your mind on God's interests, but man's" (v. 23).

Jesus was able to see clearly how Satan had tried his best to redirect His mind to focus on the horror of suffering and thus cause Him to lose sight of God's interests, which were the salvation of mankind and the joy of having accomplished redemption.

While Jesus was hanging on the cross just hours before He would die, what do you think He was doing? I believe He was still focusing on the joy after the cross was completed! These were the very hours when the fiercest battle took place between Him—the Lamb of God—and Satan, with our souls hanging in the balance.

If at that time Jesus had not concentrated His whole being on the joy afterward, He would have stepped down from the cross and wouldn't have had the strength to die. Jesus was able to face the cost it took because He maintained His focus—the joy after the cross—throughout the slow process of His death.

Because He kept this joy before Him, He was able to see, by faith, you and me and whole nations redeemed by His blood. He could see the millions of India who would praise Him and who would call upon His name for salvation. The outcome was worth the price He had to pay.

There were other people in the Bible who did exactly as Jesus did: They focused on the outcome and not on the cost.

Hebrews 11:8–10 tells us that one of these men was **Abraham.** When God called him, he left everything and became a nomad and alien in a foreign land for the rest of his life. "For he was looking for the city which has foundations, whose architect and builder is God" (Hebrews 11:10). Abraham was able to pay that kind of a price because he did not focus on the cost, but on the joy before him to arrive at this city that was made by God.

Moses was another one who did not focus on the cost. We read about him in Hebrews 11:24-26. Moses gave up the throne in Egypt and left his title, his riches and everything behind that was given to him, to suffer with the people of God, "for he was looking to the reward" (Hebrews 11:26).

He did not concentrate on the cost of having to walk around in that wilderness for 40 years, trying to lead a bunch of people who were continuously complaining, murmuring, stubborn and disobedient. Instead, Moses kept his mind on the reward that would be his afterward.

Abraham and Moses were able to look ahead by faith, just as Jesus did.

There were many other people living during the same time as Moses and Abraham, but none of them did what these two had done. The others looked at the price tag and said, "The cost is too high." They were not able to see by faith what Moses and Abraham could see, and they did not know how to set the joy before their eyes so they too could endure the cross. For example, Lot, Abraham's nephew, who at first had joined him, gave up his focus and went for an easier life in Sodom.

➢ ➢ ➢ ➢ ➢

In the days when there was no treatment for leprosy, everyone who contracted this disease became an outcast and had to live in designated leper colonies. During that time, the colonies were cut off from the outside world by high walls, and guards were posted around them to prevent anyone from coming in or going out.

There were some Moravian missionaries who had a great burden for the lepers behind these walls. Their greatest desire was that these lepers in their hopelessness could know Jesus as their Savior. But there was no way to tell them because no one was allowed to go behind these walls. Do you know what these missionaries did?

One night when the guards couldn't see them, they climbed over those walls—never to return to the outside world. They were ready to win these lepers to the Lord at the calculated cost of their own health and life.

How were they able to face and to pay such a high price? They were able to do it because, like Jesus, they had set before their eyes the joy that was to come *after* the "cross." By faith they could see, like Moses, the reward in the future. Before they ever climbed over that wall, they saw those lepers coming to the feet of Jesus.

> > > > >

I once read a story that happened during World War II in Germany. Wherever Jews were found, they were rounded up like animals and brought to Hitler's concentration camps for his final solution to the "Jewish problem"—death in the gas chambers.

There was a Jewish girl who was a born-again Christian. She had found a safe place to hide, and she knew that no one would ever find her as long as she stayed there. But day and night, she thought about her Jewish brothers and sisters in the concentration camps. She thought about the horrors and the suffering they were going through. She knew that they would die there—without knowing Jesus the Messiah.

Do you know what she did? She left her hiding place and walked into the street, confessing, "I am a Jew." As soon as she said these words, she was arrested and taken to one of the concentration camps. There she had to suffer unspeakable horrors alongside the other Jews. However, she was able to witness to many of them about the true Messiah before they were taken to the gas chambers or died of starvation and sickness.

How was this girl able to pay such a high price? Because she could see by faith, just like Jesus. She could see the joy beyond the cross when one day some of those to whom she had witnessed would stand, redeemed by the blood of Jesus, before the throne of God.

> > > > >

I don't know where the Lord intends to call you to serve Him. It might be somewhere in North India, Tibet or Bhutan. Maybe you are already at the place where God wants to invest your life for His kingdom.

Perhaps you will have to pay a high price of suffering in the days ahead. It could be that in a few years from now, we will read your name in a report that says, "Another Gospel worker died as a martyr on one of the mission fields."

Dear brother, dear sister—if you desire to be able to bear the cost so that your mission field will know Jesus, then you *must learn* to take your eyes off the price. You *must learn* to deliberately focus your mind, your heart and your eyes on the joy set before you that will be yours after the cross. Before it ever comes to pass, you *must train* yourself to see, by faith, the reward: the souls from your pioneer field washed by the blood of Jesus.

May I encourage you that in whatever the Lord asks you to do, set the joy before your eyes and you will be able to pay the price.

21

FULLY
ACCOMPLISHED

*A*s I write this book, I am 42 years old. I am surprised at how fast the years have flown by. It seems like just yesterday that our children were babies and our ministry was in its first beginnings.

Sometimes people walk up to me and express their appreciation for what our ministry is doing for the lost world. They share how astonished they are by all the things that have been accomplished.

I am happy for what God has done through His grace. But very often, when I am alone, my thoughts are just the opposite. I wonder how much of His plan God *wasn't* able to accomplish through my life. My concern is not how much I did, but how much I *didn't* do. Looking back over the years, I wonder how much time and how many opportunities I must have wasted by just being concerned about myself or because of my lack of motivation.

I am well aware that even if the Lord delays His return, half of my life has already passed. I have only half of my life left—maybe not even that much. It might be just a few more years, a few months, days or hours.

I ask myself very seriously: "With the remaining time I have left, will I be able to finish all that God has planned for my life?" I want to see Jesus and hear Him say, "You have fully accomplished what I asked you to do. Nothing was left undone."

GOD'S PURPOSE AND GOAL ARE THAT WE FINISH THE RACE!

God called us not only to follow Him, but to *fully complete* His plan, His goal and His purpose for our lives. This is expressed very clearly in the following verses:

> Be faithful *until death*, and I will give you the crown of life (Revelation 2:10).

> And he who overcomes, and he who keeps My deeds *until the end*, to him I will give authority over the nations (Revelation 2:26).

> Run in such a way that you may win (1 Corinthians 9:24).

Paul knew very well what God's purpose was for his life and what God expected him to accomplish before his death. He wrote to Timothy about this purpose: "But the Lord stood with me, and strengthened me, in order that *through me the proclamation might be fully accomplished, and that all the Gentiles might hear*" (2 Timothy 4:17). Paul had given every aspect of his life so fully to Jesus and to the goal and purpose God had shown him that before he died he could write to Timothy: "I have fought the good fight, *I have finished* the course, I have kept the faith" (2 Timothy 4:7).

Jesus also knew very well God's purpose for Him: "*That all things* which are written about Me in the Law of Moses and the Prophets and the Psalms *must be fulfilled*" (Luke 24:44). Throughout the Gospels we read this statement whenever Jesus did something: ". . . in order that the Scripture might be fulfilled . . ." At the end of His life, while He was hanging on the cross, we read, "After this, Jesus, knowing that all things had already been accomplished, in order that the Scripture might be fulfilled . . ." (John 19:28). Jesus had not left one prophecy unfulfilled or one task undone. Everything was fully accomplished. No wonder His last words—His victory cry—were, "It is finished!" (John 19:30).

Easy to Start the Race—Hard to Complete It

After the disciples saw Jesus multiply the five loaves and two fishes, it was easy for them to get excited about their call to serve such a Lord. Watching Jesus open deaf ears, give sight to the blind, cleanse the lepers and raise the dead gave them plenty of enthusiasm to proclaim Him as the Son of David and the Messiah, or Anointed One. They were quite eager to sing "Hosanna" and lay palm branches out before Him as He rode into Jerusalem.

However, it was impossible for them to maintain their excitement during the crisis they faced when Jesus was arrested, tried and executed. Of course, then came another wave of excitement when the resurrection took place and when at Pentecost the Holy Spirit came to indwell them. It caused them to embrace God's plan for their lives and the ministry to which Jesus had called them.

However, all these wonderful things were just the beginning of a long journey. What lay ahead of them? It was 20, 30, 40, 50 or more years of hard work, endless travel, intense suffering, prison, persecution and martyrs' deaths. Oh yes, there were many victories, miracles and blessings along the way. But it was a long, hard road until the end.

I believe that their first excitement would not have been sufficient to give them endurance until the end. It took more than that!

For us it takes more as well. The excitement we first experience when we go to Bible school or for outreach will not last long enough to carry us through the next 40 or 50 years of laying down our lives! It is easy to start the race but hard to finish it.

WHAT DOES IT TAKE TO FINISH?

I am aware that I am about to give an answer (or at least attempt one) to something that I have not yet completed myself. Therefore, I am looking for the "secrets" of people like Moses, Paul and of course Jesus, who all finished their races successfully.

More than anything else, we must realize that the devil will do all he can to prevent us from fully accomplishing the goal. He will allow us to do part, and then try his best to get us out of the race.

Just imagine what would have happened if Moses stopped believing God as he and the nation of Israel stood at the Red Sea with Pharaoh's army behind them or, worse, while Israel walked through the midst of the Red Sea with walls of water left and right!

Think about this: What if Paul had given up fighting his "good fight" on that ship to Rome? The storm they encountered was so violent, the situation so hopeless and desperate that Paul had every reason to give up too. If he did, we wouldn't have one letter from him in the entire New Testament.

What about Jesus? If He followed Peter's good advice not to go to the cross, we never would have salvation.

We must realize that the devil wants to stop us short of our goal. We will never know whether God purposed to use the last five years of our lives to touch a whole nation with the Gospel if we run off two weeks before it was planned to happen!

The devil will use our weaknesses, discouragements, fears,

loneliness, sin and enemies to attempt to make us give up our pursuit of God's goal. What should we do?

Don't entertain any thought or wish to get out of the race! If you give room to this thought, it will grow and overtake you.

Moses never wished himself back in Egypt and in Pharaoh's palace. Hebrews 11:25 says: "[Moses chose] rather to endure ill-treatment with the people of God."

Paul also never looked back after putting his hand to the plow, and he never considered an easier road. He wrote to the Philippians:

> But whatever things were gain to me, those things I have counted as loss for the sake of Christ (Philippians 3:7).

> . . . but one thing I do: *forgetting* what lies behind and reaching forward to what lies ahead, I *press on toward the goal* for the prize of the upward call of God in Christ Jesus (Philippians 3:13–14).

Jesus, when the devil tempted Him, could have made His life easier by accepting the shortcut the devil offered to His reign as Messiah. He could have avoided the cross altogether. Jesus immediately refused every word the devil tried to use to trick Him. He did not entertain his offer for even a moment. We must learn from Jesus to immediately reject every offer or wish that would cause us to leave the race.

Maintain a close walk with the Lord. Any kind of compromise we make in our love for the Lord and His people, our fellowship, holiness, commitment or honesty and openness is very dangerous to our spiritual health. It can cause a spiritual tiredness and carelessness that let us forget the seriousness of our calling, which in turn could lead to sin or to getting out of the battle.

Demas, Paul's co-worker, is such an example. Paul writes about him in 2 Timothy 4:10: "For Demas, having loved this present world, has deserted me and gone to Thessalonica." Demas made a compromise in his commitment and love for the Lord. All of a sudden, his call to the ministry no longer seemed so important—and he left the race.

It is absolutely vital to promptly repent from any sin that overtakes us and to immediately correct our course. Otherwise, we will find ourselves stranded on the sidelines, out of the race before we know it.

Walk in fear. Let us consider our call. Let us not take lightly that which God has entrusted to us. The blood of a lost world will be on our hands if we decide *on our own* to retire. We have a job to do that is extremely serious and has eternal consequences.

> Son of man, I have appointed you a watchman to the house of Israel; whenever you hear a word from My mouth, warn them from Me. When I say to the wicked, "You shall surely die," and you do not warn him . . . his blood I will require at your hand (Ezekiel 3:17–18).

Remember, we signed on for life, and our commitment to His call does not run out after 25 years or at age 65! *We are not finished until God says we are finished.*

Keep the vision. God has always had a vision for His people. In the Old Testament, God's vision was to have a people of His own (Deuteronomy 4:20), to give them the Promised Land (Genesis 17:8) and to make them an example and blessing to all the nations of the earth (Genesis 22:18), which was fulfilled in Jesus.

From the New Testament and on into the present, God's vision for His people has been that they would follow the cross (Luke 9:23), win a multitude of souls to Jesus from every nation and tribe (Revelation 7:9) and become a bride for the Lamb, pure and holy (Revelation 21:2).

The Bible says, "Where there is no vision, the people perish" (Proverbs 29:18, KJV). This is very true for our physical as well as our spiritual lives. Any improvement in society, in the church or in our personal lives requires a vision. Otherwise, no change, no effort, no improvement will ever happen. Consider these examples:

Moses had the vision to free Israel from slavery, take them out of Egypt and bring them to the Promised Land.

Joshua's vision was to cross the Jordan River and conquer Canaan.

Nehemiah's vision was to rebuild the broken-down wall of Jerusalem, while **Ezra** had the vision to rebuild the temple.

Jesus' vision was to die for our sins, and **Paul's** vision was to take the Gospel to the Gentiles.

Each of these men faced tremendous odds, yet amazingly they succeeded and accomplished the tasks they set out to do. When we read about their lives, we find that all the difficulties of the world, enormous struggles, suffering and persecution couldn't stop them from fulfilling their mission.

What gave them the drive, the energy and the burden to go on when all looked so hopeless? It was their vision that kept them going. You see, a vision always comes first, which will then produce a burden. This burden will cause you to go forward and fulfill the vision.

Look closely at the life of any leader who is doing something great for the Lord. You will find without exception that each one has a vision and, through it, a tremendous burden to fulfill that vision. Where does this vision come from? God gave it to them!

It was not Moses' idea to free Israel or Paul's idea to take the Gospel to the Gentiles. These visions were first born in the heart of God. He then searched for someone with a willing heart whom He could call, impart this vision and then fulfill it through him. We read this truth in Ezekiel 22:30: "And I searched for a man among them who should build up the wall and stand in the gap before Me for the land, that I should not destroy it; but I found no one."

Each of the men I have mentioned accepted God's vision and made it their own. They allowed God to work mightily through them until it was fulfilled.

In the very same way, when God calls you to serve Him, He will offer you a vision and a purpose for your life and ministry. You must not only accept this vision, but make it your *own* as well. It might be a small vision at first, which will expand and unfold as you walk with Him.

It must be your highest priority to keep this vision alive, because it is the energy, the drive and the source of the burden you need to fulfill your calling. You cannot afford to let it die, be buried under other things or replaced by the attractions of the world. Where there is no vision, the people perish; and without vision, your call will perish as well!

There are quite a number of people in the Bible who lost their vision. We can learn from their lives what will happen to us, our calling and our ministry if we ever lose ours.

The people of Israel left Egypt with the vision to go to Canaan in the shortest time possible. Yet when they arrived at the border of the Promised Land, they found fortified cities and giants there. At that moment they lost their vision and decided to go back to Egypt. The result was that they walked in circles in the desert for 40 years and finally died there, never reaching their destination.

Orpah and Ruth, two Moabite girls, had the vision to go to Bethlehem with Naomi to start a new life. However, somewhere along the way, **Orpah** lost her vision when she thought about her relatives, home and country. She never reached Bethlehem. She also never received and shared any of the blessings that the God of Israel gave to Ruth. Ruth not only became the wife of Boaz and had a good life, but she also became an ancestor of King David and Jesus.

When **Jonah** lost his vision to obey the Lord and go to Nineveh, he ended up having "fish trouble" and in the process delayed God's plans and His timetable.

God had given **King Saul** the vision and the promise that if he was faithful, his kingdom would be established forever. However, Saul lost his vision and disobeyed God. The end result was that his kingdom was taken from him.

Next to the power of the Holy Spirit, your vision is the most important tool you have received from the Lord to enable you to complete your mission. As you walk along, the devil will do his best to rob you of your vision through fear, the love for the things of the world, glamorous offers catered to your ego and distractions by other good things. Don't ever let anything rob you of your vision! You must keep it at any cost. Once you let go of it, you are a candidate for walking off of the racetrack.

If your vision has faded or you have lost it altogether, you must immediately get it rekindled. Remove all the distractions from your life that have caused you to lose sight of your vision. Seek God in prayer and stay before Him until your vision is back in your heart.

Always remember, you will only attempt to accomplish that for which you have a vision.

Be determined. For Paul, it was not an accident that he remained faithful until the end and was able to finish God's plan for his life. You see, very early in his Christian life, Paul made God's purpose and goal his purpose and goal. He determined and purposed in his heart that he would allow nothing and no one to stop his pursuit of it until all was fully accomplished:

> But I do not consider my life of any account as dear to myself, in order that I may finish my course, and the ministry which I received from the Lord Jesus, to testify solemnly of the gospel of the grace of God (Acts 20:24).

Our determination is more important and more powerful than we think. It shapes our thoughts and actions and gives us a willingness to endure until the goal is reached. There is a song that has often challenged me to keep up my commitment. The words go like this: "I am determined to be invincible until He has finished His purpose in me."

Let us, like Paul, determine today that we will be faithful, obedient and invincible through Jesus. We will not be satisfied with less than fulfilling our goal. We will not give up after we fail or stumble. We will hold still for the Holy Spirit to work on our heart. We will complete our race and win.

We must make this determination before our body gets tired, old and weary and before the pressures of life bear down on us. You see, when we are young, we have enough energy to compensate for hardships. Later on in life, however, we can no longer draw on our physical strength to keep us going. We can only cling to our determination that through His grace we will not give up, regardless, until His goal is fully accomplished through our lives.

Stand on His promises, and count on His grace and power. All our efforts and our best determination will not be enough to keep us in the race that is set before us. Unless God gives us His grace and His power, we have no chance at all to make it. He has to be the One who lives and accomplishes His purpose through us.

All that is required of us is to allow Him to do so. Our faith activates His power and allows Him to fulfill every promise He has made in His Word. Here are some of these promises that will encourage us to be determined not to give up until God's purpose is accomplished:

I am with you always, even to the end of the age (Matthew 28:20).

For I am confident of this very thing, that He who began a

good work in you will perfect it until the day of Christ Jesus (Philippians 1:6).

For I know whom I have believed and I am convinced that He is able to guard what I have entrusted to Him until that day (2 Timothy 1:12).

COMPLETE THE RACE FOR OTHERS WHO FOLLOW

It is frightening to see how few servants of God fully complete their race. It seems as though the dropout rate becomes greater and greater as the race crosses the halfway mark and winds down toward the finish line. The last 100 meters are always the hardest. Each runner is exhausted, and his muscles are aching. Yet he must speed up one more time and squeeze the last possible ounce of energy out of his tired body. Only if he is able to cross that white line has he successfully completed the race.

Why is it that so many Christian leaders, as well as believers, seem to have trouble completing their race with the same dedication and testimony as they ran it the first 20, 30 or 40 years?

I believe the reason might be that when we are in the battle for a long time, we come to a point where we just desire to relax, to sit down a while and to get out from under the pressure. We want to have time for our families and friends. As we get older, we may also feel that we deserve a little easier life, especially because we've done more than others. At this point it is easy to lose our concentration, and we stumble or slow down considerably. The enemy takes advantage of our loss of focus and sidetracks us by showing us the joys of an easier life.

I am not at all saying that a 75-year-old Gospel worker should walk as far and carry the same heavy load of literature as a 25-year-old. No, the Lord knows our frame, our age and our physical strength, and He considers them all. What I am talking about is this: We must keep the fire alive in our hearts and our goal set before us.

It is very, very important to God that we do not lose the race on the home stretch. You see, we do not complete the race just for ourselves, but for others as well. God is not only concerned that we fulfill His plan but that we become an example for others, showing them how to run and how to finish the race. He wants to be able to point to our lives and tell those who have just started, "Follow his or her example. Learn from him, and you too will fully accomplish My plan." This intent of God to use us as examples becomes very clear when we read Hebrews 13:7: "Remember those who led you, who spoke the word of God to you; and considering the outcome of their way of life, imitate their faith."

Paul was so sure he had kept the faith and his commitment that he could tell the Corinthian Christians, "Be imitators of me, just as I also am of Christ" (1 Corinthians 11:1).

To Timothy he said, "And the things which you have heard from me . . . these entrust to faithful men. . . . But you followed my teaching, conduct, purpose, faith, patience, love, perseverance, persecutions, sufferings . . ." (2 Timothy 2:2, 3:10-11).

And to the Philippians he said, "Brethren, join in following my example, and observe those who walk according to the pattern you have in us. . . . The things you have learned and received and heard and seen in me, practice these things; and the God of peace shall be with you" (Philippians 3:17, 4:9).

Others look at us to draw strength and instruction from our lives. What do they see?

A few days ago it occurred to me that no one in our ministry actually saw my life when I was 19, 20 or 21 years old. None of them witnessed my excitement, my love for the Lord, my boldness or anything I did at that time. There are maybe three or four who have known me for the past 10 years, but the rest of them have only seen my life for less than 4 to 5 years, and some just a few months.

They know nothing about my spiritual background. What I did or who I was 20 years ago does not have much meaning for them. All they can see is what I portray and live right now before their eyes.

When they look at my life at this moment, what will they see? How is my excitement, my determination, my vision, my faithfulness, my love for the Lord? Am I still in the race? Am I still looking ahead?

I remember a radio preacher telling his audience that he only uses examples in his preaching of believers and leaders who had already died. The dropout rate from the race is so high, and he wants to make sure that those he mentions have no chance left to ruin their testimony.

Over the years I have felt disappointed more than once by well-known leaders, pastors or missionaries who changed so completely in their dedication to Christ that they became greedy for money, jealous of others' success and position or very liberal in their view of sin. I do not want to judge them, but I want to take it as a warning: If we are not careful, we will discourage many believers from completing their races. Others need to see us cross the finish line, so they too will have the courage to endure until the end.

Help Each Other to Complete the Race

A few years ago, a missionary told me, "My wife asks me to stay home now. She says, 'This is my old age—give the ministry to younger ones and let us spend these last few years in peace.' "

I can understand her desire and tiredness very well. They both worked so hard for all those years and have done so much for the kingdom. Now his wife would like to have a more quiet life, with less responsibility and more time for each other.

When we meet someone who is getting weary and tired in the race or losing his concentration and starting to struggle and stumble, we are given orders to help him get back on track. This is not done by judging, condemning or criticizing, but by love that carries someone else's burden.

> Now we who are strong ought to bear the weaknesses of those without strength and not just please ourselves (Romans 15:1).

> Bear one another's burdens, and thus fulfill the law of Christ (Galatians 6:2).

> Therefore encourage one another, and build up one another (1 Thessalonians 5:11).

During an international athletic competition, a race took place that perfectly illustrates what it means to help someone else fully accomplish the goal. Two runners were ahead of everyone else, and the finish line was already in sight. The spectators were sure that the first runner would definitely receive the gold medal, because he was far enough ahead of the second runner.

However, just meters before the finish line, to everyone's horror, the first runner began to stagger and stumble and finally fell down, completely exhausted on the sidelines. The crowd cheered to encourage him to get up, but it was useless. He desperately tried to get on his feet, but all his strength had left him.

In a few moments the race would be over. All the other runners would pass him by and cross the finish line, while he could only watch helplessly. He would not only lose the medal, but the records would forever show that he had never finished the race.

Just as the second runner passed him by, sure to win first place now, something totally unexpected happened that made the crowd hold its breath. The second runner suddenly left his track, ran over to the sidelines and pulled up the first runner from the ground. He laid the exhausted man's arm around his shoulder and placed his own arm around his waist. To the cheering of the crowd, he dragged his stranded opponent with him toward the white line. They struggled and stumbled, but they crossed the finish line together to share the prize.

⟩ ⟩ ⟩ ⟩ ⟩ OTHER BOOKS BY GISELA YOHANNAN

BROKEN FOR A PURPOSE

"Why do trials come my way?" Drawing from her own walk with the Lord, Gisela shares how to find strength in God's presence and overcome seasons of testing so that Christ's life flows through you.

DEAR SISTER,

Through a series of letters written over seven years, Gisela shares candidly about the events of her life and ministry—both joys and sorrows—and how the Lord has been faithful through it all. *Dear Sister,* holds out to you the promise of fresh beginnings, of new mercies every morning and of hope in your walk with Jesus.

Order online at www.gfa.org

 GOSPEL FOR ASIA

After 2,000 years of Christianity, how can it be that nearly 3 billion people are still unreached with the Gospel? How long must they wait?

This is why Gospel for Asia exists.

More than 25 years ago, God specifically called us to invest our lives to reach the most unreached of the Indian subcontinent through training and sending out native missionaries.

Gospel for Asia (GFA) is a church-planting organization dedicated to reaching the most unreached in the 10/40 Window. Our 16,500 pastors and missionaries serve full-time to plant churches in India, Nepal, China, Bhutan, Myanmar, Sri Lanka, Bangladesh, Laos, Vietnam and Thailand.

Native missionaries are highly effective because they work in their own or a similar culture. They already know, or can easily learn, the language, customs and culture of the people to whom they minister. They don't need visas, and they live economically at the same level as their neighbors. These advantages make them one of the fastest and most effective ways to get the Gospel to the millions who are still waiting to be reached. By God's grace, GFA missionaries have established more than 30,000 churches and mission stations to date.*

However, the young, economically weak Asian Church and her missionaries can't do it alone. The enormous task of evangelizing nearly 3 billion people takes the help of the whole Body of Christ worldwide.

That is why GFA offers those who cannot go themselves the opportunity to become senders and prayer partners of native missionaries—together fulfilling the Great Commission and sharing in the eternal harvest of souls.

To find out more information about Gospel for Asia or to receive a free copy of K.P. Yohannan's best-selling book *Revolution in World Missions*, visit our website at www.gfa.org or contact one of our offices near you.

* As of 2007

UNITED STATES   1800 Golden Trail Court, Carrollton, TX 75010
        Toll free: 1-800-WIN-ASIA   Email: info@gfa.org

AUSTRALIA   P.O. Box 3587, Village Fair, Toowoomba QLD 4350
        Phone: (07) 4632-4131   Email: infoaust@gfa.org

CANADA   245 King Street E, Stoney Creek, ON L8G 1L9
        Toll free: 1-888-WIN-ASIA   Email: infocanada@gfa.org

GERMANY   Postfach 13 60, 79603 Rheinfelden (Baden)
        Phone: 07623 79 74 77   Email: infogermany@gfa.org

KOREA   P.O. Box 984, Yeouido, Seoul 150-609
        Toll free: 82-80-801-0191   Email: infokorea@gfa.or.kr

NEW ZEALAND   P.O. Box 302580, North Harbour, North Shore City 0751
        Toll free: 0508-918-918   Email: infonz@gfa.org

SOUTH AFRICA   P.O. Box 28880, Sunridge Park, Port Elizabeth 6008
        Phone: 041 360-0198   Email: infoza@gfa.org

UNITED KINGDOM   P.O. Box 166, Winterscale House, YORK YO10 5WA
        Freephone: 0800 032 8717   Email: infouk@gfa.org

CHARTER ECFA MEMBER

A higher standard.
A higher purpose.